What others say about this book

'Designed to work seamlessly with our Business Model and Value Proposition Canvases, the Market Opportunity Navigator, proposed by Marc and Sharon, will help entrepreneurs and innovators to commercialise technologies. You will enjoy discovering highly practical worksheets, maps and dartboards of tremendous interest if you want to better identify, evaluate and strategise market opportunities. Let yourself be charmed by the toolkit and the case studies, along with the thoughts of Marc and Sharon.'

Alex Osterwalder and Yves Pigneur, authors of the bestseller *Business Model Generation*

'When two internationally-known experts in entrepreneurship write a "how to" book on market opportunities for entrepreneurs, it is bound to be a very valuable book indeed. Marc Gruber and Sharon Tal have created just the right book for first-time and experienced entrepreneurs. It contains both step-by-step plans and very valuable tips on identifying market opportunities – an invaluable complement to both the Lean Start-up Process and the Business Model Canvas!'

Eric von Hippel, T. Wilson Professor of Innovation, MIT Sloan School of Management

'From entrepreneurship thought leaders comes this innovative step-by-step guide to thinking through the market essentials of an opportunity. Rather than relying on generic examples or others' stories, the authors put the reader in the driver's seat by encouraging him or her to generate, evaluate and prepare to act on their own opportunities. I can't think of a more practically useful entrepreneurship book.'

Dean A. Shepherd, Ray and Milann Siegfried Professor of Entrepreneurship, Mendoza College of Business, Notre Dame University

'Gruber and Tal have crafted a visually exciting way for entrepreneurs to identify and analyse their opportunities, before they dive into execution. This book pairs nicely with the Business Model Canvas and Lean Startup. Best of all, it also tells you how to focus, and what NOT to do!'
Henry Chesbrough, UC Berkeley Haas School of Business professor, and author of Open Innovation.

'Using thoughtful research and compelling examples, Where to Play provides important guidance on how to balance focus and flexibility when launching a new venture. It builds on the Lean Startup model by providing meaningful insights on what markets to address first.'
Tina Seelig, Professor of the Practice, Stanford School of Engineering

'Where to Play attacks head-on one of the most difficult questions any aspiring entrepreneur must answer: "Which target market should I serve?" It's visual, easy-to-apply, and full of common-sense. If I were starting a business today, I wouldn't leave the starting blocks without it!'
John Mullins, Professor, London Business School; best selling author, The New Business Road Test and The Customer-Funded Business

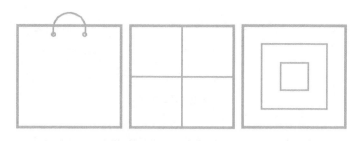

WHERE TO PLAY

WHERE TO PLAY

3 steps for discovering your most valuable
market opportunities

Marc Gruber and Sharon Tal

 **Pearson**

Harlow, England • London • New York • Boston • San Francisco • Toronto • Sydney • Dubai • Singapore • Hong Kong
Tokyo • Seoul • Taipei • New Delhi • Cape Town • São Paulo • Mexico City • Madrid • Amsterdam • Munich • Paris • Milan

Pearson Education Limited
KAO Two
KAO Park
Harlow CM17 9NA
United Kingdom
Tel: +44 (0)1279 623623
Web: www.pearson.com/uk

First edition published 2017 (print and electronic)

ISBN: 978-1-292-17892-9 (print)
         978-1-292-17893-6 (PDF)
         978-1-292-17894-3 (ePub)

British Library Cataloguing-in-Publication Data
A catalogue record for the print edition is available from the British Library

Library of Congress Cataloging-in-Publication Data
A catalog record for the print edition is available from the Library of Congress

Text design by Dana Shimoni
Cover design by Two Associates based on an idea by Dana Shimoni
Print edition typeset in 9.5/15 pt Open Sans by iEnergizer Aptara®, Ltd.

NOTE THAT ANY PAGE CROSS REFERENCES REFER TO THE PRINT EDITION

In this book you will find

About the authors

Where to Play presents a new business tool with a solid underpinning called the Market Opportunity Navigator. It was developed based on over 15 years of rigorous research, combined with years of practical experience in consulting and teaching budding entrepreneurs. Hundreds of cases, from different industries and countries, were studied and analysed as we developed the underlying logic of the Market Opportunity Navigator. The result is a simple and appealing tool, which has the right amount of depth to help you make solid decisions.

Marc is a world-leading researcher in the domain of innovation, entrepreneurship and technology commercialisation. He is Vice President for Innovation at the Swiss Federal Institute of Technology (EPFL) in Lausanne, Switzerland, where he also heads the Chair of Entrepreneurship and Technology Commercialisation. He works as the Deputy Editor for the #1 empirical research journal in management, the *Academy of Management Journal*. He received multiple 'Thought Leader' awards for his breakthrough research. Marc is actively engaged in teaching, consulting and executive training programmes in Europe, the US and Asia, and regularly acts as a jury member in start-up and corporate entrepreneurship competitions across Europe.

Sharon is one of the co-founders and former executive director of the Entrepreneurship Centre at the Technion, Israel Institute of Technology, and a well-recognised lecturer on marketing for high-tech start-ups. She conducts seminars and workshops on a regular basis to students and start-ups, and serves as a mentor in many organisations that aim to help budding entrepreneurs. Sharon has vast experience in marketing and has served as a marketing manager for firms in several industries. She also has extensive experience in strategy consulting. Her PhD research investigated the market entry decisions of hundreds of start-ups and their consequences on firm performance and flexibility.

Acknowledgements

We are grateful to the following for permission to reproduce copyright material:

Figures
Part 3.3 from *Business Model Generation: A Handbook for Visionaries, Game Changers, and Challengers*. (Osterwalder, A., Pigneur, Y., In Clark, T. & Smith, A. 2010). Courtesy of Strategyzer (https://strategyzer.com); Part 3.3 from *Value Proposition Design: How to Create Products and Services Customers Want*, Hoboken Wiley (Osterwalder, A., Pigneur, Y., Bernarda, G. & Smith, A. 2015). Courtesy of Strategyzer (https://strategyzer.com).

Photographs and artwork
The publisher would like to thank the following for their kind permission to reproduce their photographs and artwork:

Saar Yoskovitch/Gal Shaul/Augury: 37, 46, 52, 55, 67, 75, 78, 81, 83, 88, 91, 94, 96, 108, 131, 141, 150, 152; FLYABILITY SA: 155; FujiFilm Holdings Corporation: 51; Marc Gruber/Sharon Tal: 22, 32, 130, 168, 188, 204.

'The entrepreneur's dilemma: focus, focus, focus – but on WHAT?'
David Roth, Forbes Magazine

'The hardest thing when you think about focusing. You think focusing is about saying "Yes". No. Focusing is about saying "No".'
Steve Jobs, Apple co-founder

'The thing about inventing is you have to be both stubborn and flexible, more or less simultaneously. The hard part is figuring out when to be which!'
Jeff Bezos, Amazon founder

'You have to be prepared to see the better idea when it arrives. And the hardest part of that is often discarding your old idea.'
Paul Graham, Y Combinator co-founder

If you've ever felt these challenges, this book is for you . . .

Where to Play presents the Market Opportunity Navigator- a tool that will help you:

Discover promising market opportunities

Evaluate their value

Set your strategic focus smartly

To make sure you're running in the right direction and remain agile, without losing your focus!

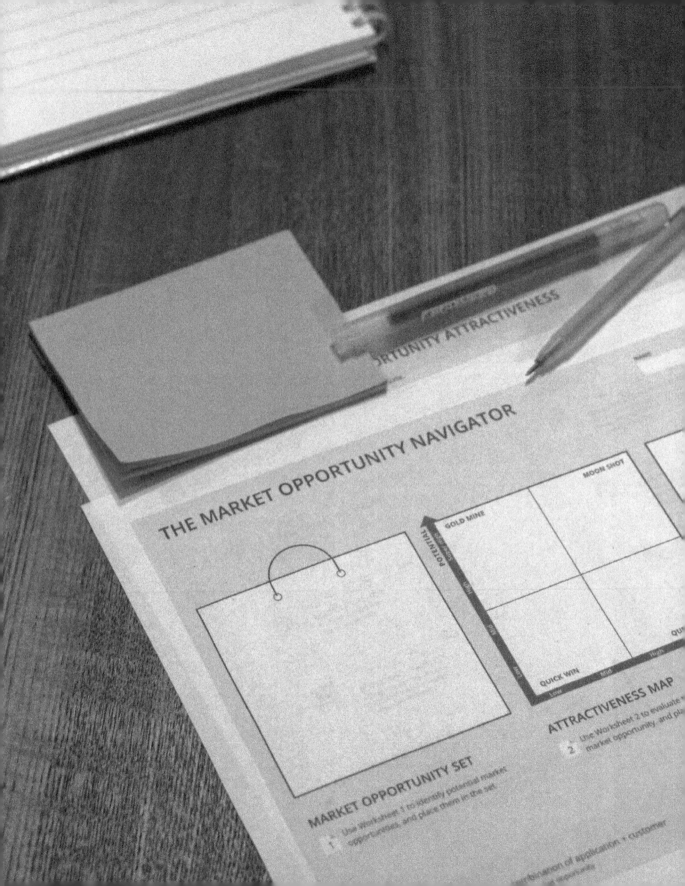

Overview

1.1 Are you running in the right direction?

Commercialising innovative ideas is a constant run.
It requires immense efforts, as you attempt to move forward and make progress on your way . . . while facing one hurdle after the other. And it's not just simply running . . . in fact, entrepreneurs and innovators are trained to run fast. Time can be one of your greatest enemies when new products or services are waiting to be adopted, and speed is seen as critical to successful innovation.

Yet, running, and even running fast, may simply be useless if you are not running in the right direction! If you are not pursuing a valuable market opportunity, or not playing in the right field, you are wasting your time, energy and resources . . . and those of others, too!

Finding the right direction, however, is not obvious at all. Your unique resources and abilities can address different needs, for different sets of customers, thereby creating several potential market opportunities for your venture – or a set of possible paths in your entrepreneurial race!

So before you run fast, make sure you are running in the right direction, because . . .

Different paths lead to different results
Market opportunities differ in their value creation potential and thus in your ability to generate sales and become successful.

Your market choice imprints your venture
Your market choice will shape many aspects of your emerging venture. It will not be easy to un-do, especially when significant investments are required.

Have you been asking yourself . . .

- ☐ How can I identify blockbuster opportunities?
- ☐ Did I miss out on any?
- ☐ How do I know what's the most valuable option if there is so much uncertainty out there?
- ☐ How can I let go of seemingly promising opportunities?
- ☐ Should I pursue several opportunities in parallel?

The Market Opportunity Navigator will support your market choice and help you to systematically uncover the most valuable market opportunities.

In short: it will help you to make sure that you are running in the right direction.

Are you locking yourself into one direction?

Once you have chosen your direction, you also need to make sure that you can remain agile, without slowing your pace. Your efforts, your resources, your attention – they should all be focused on advancing your chosen path, but at the same time you need to develop your capabilities in a way that would allow you to redirect your route.

That is because unforeseeable things may happen: despite your best, diligent efforts in choosing the most promising path, you may reach a startling dead-end and will need to pivot; you may also uncover a new, more attractive opportunity and consider its potential; or, down the road you may simply want to exploit your next growth options in the most efficient and effective manner. In short: new junctions, which are currently unforeseeable, may appear along your way, and you must make sure that you make the most out of them.

So, what does it mean to remain agile while running in your chosen direction? It means that you understand your options and keep some of them open now – so that you avoid locking yourself out of other interesting directions in the future.

When you consciously keep selected options open, you can, for example, create a more modularised technology, cast a wider intellectual property (IP) net or even pick a brand name that would lend itself to redirection. In short, it would help you to develop your resources and capabilities in a way that would allow for greater flexibility down the road.

Especially for start-ups, being able to focus while remaining agile is crucial. If you are not open to alternative paths while concentrating your available resources, and can't handle change or adaptation efficiently, you may simply lose the race . . .

The innovator's challenge: focus and be agile.

Have you been asking yourself . . .

- If market choice is so important how can I hedge my bets?
- How can I focus sharply yet stay flexible at the same time?
- What shall I do with new information that cracks my confidence in our chosen path?
- How can I deal with the next junction in our road?

The Market Opportunity Navigator will help you to strategise your opportunities and decide which options you should keep open as backups or for additional growth, so that you can stay both focused and agile at the same time.

Three steps to support your market opportunity choice

The book will take you through three steps that are necessary for designing your market opportunity strategy and choosing where to play:

I. Search broadly

Which market opportunities exist for us?

It is important to understand your terrain and uncover potential paths before you start running. Step 1 will guide you on how to search systematically and broadly for market opportunities in order to create a varied set of options.

II. Assess deeply

What are the most attractive market opportunities for us?

Next, it is essential to assess your options and understand their pros and cons. Step 2 will guide you on how to evaluate opportunities, so that you can estimate and compare their attractiveness in an unbiased manner.

III. Strategise smartly

What market opportunities should we focus on?

This is where choosing smartly comes in: it's not only about focusing on the most promising option, but also about remaining agile. Step 3 will guide you on how to build your Agile Focus Strategy, so that you can mitigate your risks and increase the value you can create – with minimum effort!

Overall, this book will take you by the hand as you progress from:

The many possible options . . .	to recognising patterns and distinctions among your options . . .	to designing a promising strategy

Manage your commercialisation effort in the face of uncertainty

The Agile Focus Strategy clearly defines the market opportunities that you will pursue now, and the opportunities that you will keep open as Backup or Growth Options, so that you can manage your start-up with foresight and agility, while facing uncertainty.

This smart portfolio will be essential for running in the right direction and for remaining agile. Eventually, it will have significant implications on how you build and design your firm.

So before you . . .

- Develop your technology
- File your patents
- Recruit new employees
- Engage your stakeholders
- Nurture your company culture
- Pick a brand name
- Design your marketing materials

☑ **Make sure to apply the Market Opportunity Navigator and design your Agile Focus Strategy!**

Enhance your value creation potential

The three steps of the Market Opportunity Navigator will successfully . . .

Support your decision making

Identify valuable opportunities and make an informed decision for enhancing your value creation potential – one that is less vulnerable to biases and that is not based mainly on intuition.

Establish a shared language

Communicate, share and debate with your team members and stakeholders, to enhance your learning, to showcase your potential and to reach agreements more easily.

Offer guidance over time

Trace back, track and update your decision over time, at any junction along your path, or whenever new information puts your strategy in doubt. Just like navigators that you know from other walks in life, this will help you to re-calculate your route if necessary. It's your learning companion.

The Market Opportunity Navigator works for . . .

Start-ups

Faced with uncertainty, start-ups often struggle to find their path to success. They need to make sure to focus on pursuing the most valuable opportunity on one hand, and hedge their bets on the other – and all with limited resources. The Market Opportunity Navigator will help entrepreneurs to identify and map their options as they progress along their entrepreneurial journey, and to choose a path that can lead them to success.

Established organisations

Established firms often struggle in creating the most value from their existing assets and in identifying opportunities for new growth. The Market Opportunity Navigator will help established firms to identify the next BIG thing and to manage their innovation funnel smartly, so that their entrepreneurial endeavours are better positioned for success.

Technology Transfer Offices

Research institutes often struggle with how to commercialise or spin out innovative technologies stemming from their laboratories. Finding potential applications and customers for these inventions is challenging, yet of key importance for these offices. It will support their decision to patent an innovation and can help them understand how – and to whom – they shall license it.

Investors

Investors are constantly looking for promising businesses. While they do want to invest in a specific market opportunity, they also greatly appreciate the value of agility. They can use the Navigator as a screening tool – to evaluate the attractiveness of an opportunity and, if it proves to be interesting, to encourage the development of a smart portfolio around it.

Educators and accelerators

No matter if you are teaching entrepreneurship or technology commercialisation in universities, or if you are accompanying budding entrepreneurs in an accelerator or an incubator: this book provides a suite of important tools that clearly lays out all the major considerations of this process, and all in an easy-to-apply form.

Use the Market Opportunity Navigator with other business tools

The Market Opportunity Navigator is an easy-to-apply business tool that helps you in systematically identifying and rigorously assessing potential opportunities as you choose which options to focus on. It not only gives you the ability to deliberately plan your strategy but also to reflect and adjust it as you progress through your learning journey.

To make this learning process broad and complete, we recommend that you use the Market Opportunity Navigator together with other key methods and business tools. Specifically, the Navigator is designed to work seamlessly with the Business Model and Value Proposition Canvases, created by Alexander Osterwalder and Yves Pigneur, and with the Lean Start-up Methodology, created by Eric Ries and Steve Blank.

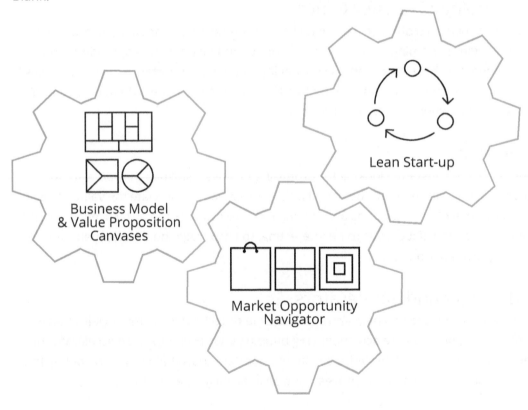

Business Model & Value Proposition Canvases

Lean Start-up

Market Opportunity Navigator

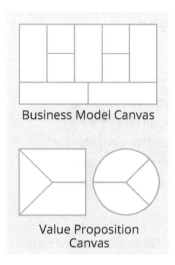

Business Model Canvas

Value Proposition
Canvas

The Business Model Canvas and the Value Proposition Canvas offer valuable frameworks that help you to plan your strategy in order to create value for your customers and for your firm.

The Navigator – which provides the macro view of the landscape of opportunities – adds an essential level of analysis to the micro-planning of the Business Model and the Value Proposition Canvases. Together, these three tools reinforce each other to provide the comprehensive planning that is required for finding the most fertile ground for your endeavour.

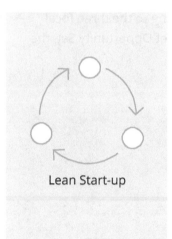

Lean Start-up

The Lean Start-up Methodology offers an important validation process for discovering and developing customers through rapid market testing and continuous pivoting.

The combination of the Navigator with the Lean Start-up Methodology allows for a powerful process of validating a winning strategy: the Navigator provides an on-going tool for planning, reflecting and adjusting as you go through rapid Lean cycles of learning and makes sure that you will always keep track of the broad picture in addition to the path that you are currently testing.

This suite of business tools helps you in understanding fundamental questions in entrepreneurship and innovation in a manner that none of the tools by itself would allow you to. The whole is greater than the sum of its parts. **Use this powerful combination to set your strategy for success.**

Turn to Chapter 3.3 for a more detailed explanation on how you can reap the greatest benefit from this suite of business tools!

1.2 The Market Opportunity Navigator in a nutshell

The Market Opportunity Navigator is designed to help you master your market opportunity strategy and find out where to play. It offers a structured and easy to apply framework covering the three main questions that you need to consider for setting a smart strategy: (I) Which market opportunities exist for us? (II) What are the most attractive market opportunities for us? (III) What market opportunities should we focus on?

The Navigator takes you through these questions, step by step. Dedicated worksheets will help you to find the best answers, and to depict their outcome in a visual manner, so that choice becomes more apparent. Corresponding to the three focal questions, the Navigator is comprised of three parts: the Market Opportunity Set, the Attractiveness Map and the Agile Focus Dartboard.

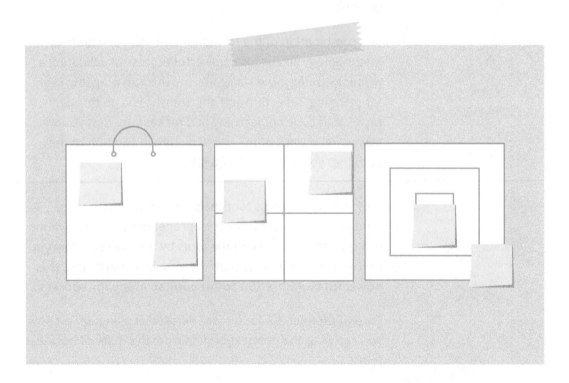

Market Opportunity Set

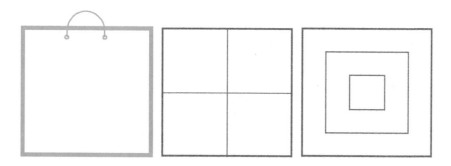

What is it?

The set of potential market opportunities that you can address with your core resources and capabilities. These can be varied options, related to different types of needs for different types of customers.

Why is it important?

Market opportunities can vastly differ in their attractiveness. A varied set of market opportunities is an asset in and of itself, as it increases your chances of focusing on the most promising option. It also provides the basis for a Plan B, if required, and for unlocking new growth opportunities over time. 'Look before you leap' is therefore the first step for setting a smart strategy.

How is it done?

To discover valuable market opportunities, assess the generic functionalities of your core abilities, to understand what other applications you can create with them for different types of customers.

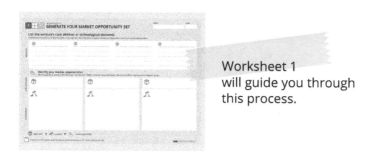

Worksheet 1
will guide you through
this process.

Attractiveness Map

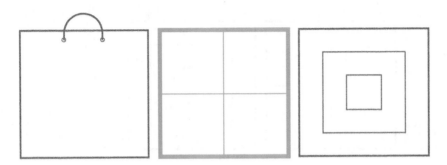

What is it?

Because market opportunities can vastly differ in their attractiveness, you need to understand their value. The Attractiveness Map allows you to visually depict the evaluation of your market opportunities, so you can better grasp their upsides and downsides, and compare them with each other.

Why is it important?

This visualisation helps you in determining your most valuable options, at a given point in time, so that you can make an informed decision about your Primary Market Opportunity – one that relies less on intuition or suffers from the biases that we all have.

How is it done?

The attractiveness of possible market opportunities is based on their value creation potential and on the challenge encountered in capturing this value. The rating of each option on both dimensions results in its location on the map.

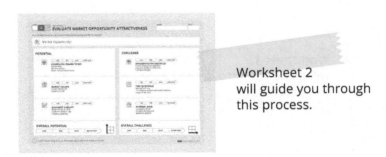

Worksheet 2 will guide you through this process.

Agile Focus Dartboard

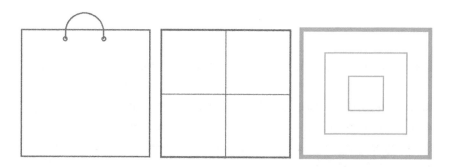

What is it?

The Dartboard depicts your Agile Focus Strategy. This strategy balances the tension between focus and flexibility, by consciously keeping open other market options: those that will allow you to mitigate your risk and increase your value with minimum effort.

Why is it important?

The Agile Focus Strategy enables you to hedge your risk and to leverage your competences at the same time, thus allocating your resources more effectively and avoiding a potentially fatal lock-in. The Agile Focus Strategy has significant implications for how you build and design your venture.

How is it done?

After choosing your Primary Market Opportunity, analyse which other options are suitable for backup or for growth, based on their attractiveness and their relatedness to your primary market. This analysis can help you decide which options should be pursued in parallel, kept open for later stages or put aside for now.

Worksheet 3
will guide you through
this process.

Before you roll up your sleeves . . .

1. It's a process

Applying the Navigator is a process that requires attention and time. Dedicating this time is often counterintuitive to the common 'just do it' tendency of entrepreneurs and innovators. Getting products out there and iterating as they go seems like a better use of time. However, thinking thoroughly through your business and unearthing important variables beforehand can actually get you on the road to success quicker and cheaper . . .

Appreciate the process, not just the outcome

Although the Market Opportunity Navigator is designed to help you set a smart strategy, the learning process to get there is just as important! It helps you figure out the strengths of your business, your competitive landscape, your customers and your obstacles. You can use the Navigator's process to clarify your assumptions about a market opportunity and to gradually turn them into facts. So don't try to make any short cuts or skip some parts of the process. The knowledge you will gather is indispensable!

Make it as iterative as possible

It may seem like a linear process – yet it is not. You will go back and forth between steps, as more knowledge is accumulated and new market opportunities are discovered.

Make it a habit

The Market Opportunity Navigator will help you in navigating through the initial market entry decision, but also beyond it! Things may constantly evolve and new parameters may require additional attention. Make the Market Opportunity Navigator a constant companion – you can capture your ongoing learning and updated situations. If strategic changes are required, you will easily see them! The Navigator will help you to see a better idea when it arrives, and to overcome the challenge of discarding your old one.

2. Use the three steps according to your own needs

Although we portray the Navigator's process in a structured and staged manner, it is actually possible – and sometimes even more useful – to apply the Navigator in a different order, or simply use individual parts according to your specific questions or dilemmas.

It's possible to start from different entry points

You can start using the Market Opportunity Navigator at different stages, and use different steps, depending on what you already know and what you have already decided. For example, you may use it to compare potential market opportunities, but not to generate alternatives, or to build a smart portfolio around a target market that you already pursue.

Market pull

Some firms may start with the intention to address a specific market need. This approach is typically called 'market pull'. If your firm falls in this category, you will find great value in the Market Opportunity Navigator as it allows you to evaluate your initial target market. If it proves to be a worthwhile opportunity, you can then build an Agile Focus Strategy around it. If it turns out to be a weak opportunity, the Market Opportunity Navigator will assist you in discovering more valuable fields to play in!

Technology push

Some firms may start with a technological invention and search for potential uses for their technology. They are typically called 'technology push' firms. If your firm falls in this category, you will find great value in the Market Opportunity Navigator as it allows you to discover possible market opportunities, stemming from your innovation, to evaluate them and to develop your Agile Focus Strategy.

3. Work efficiently

Remember that the Navigator provides you with the cornerstone questions that need to be addressed as you figure out where to play, but it does not provide the answers. Here are some important tips to help you search for answers in a more effective manner:

Avoid 'paralysis by analysis'

Paralysis by analysis is a well-known phenomenon. It refers to managers who are reluctant to make important decisions before gathering all the information that they could possibly get. While our framework urges you to collect comprehensive data before setting your strategy, we also urge you to stop at some reasonable point. Uncertainty can never really fade completely. Be prepared to base your decision on an 'informed and educated intuition' rather than on a complete set of data. The fine line between under- and over-analysis is a bit illusive, so you should be aware of it.

Be aware of your biases

As human beings, we are never an empty table. We usually approach tasks with our prior beliefs, tendencies, passions etc. This is normal. Yet, don't use the Market Opportunity Navigator to simply rationalise your intuition. Try to be as objective as possible and to base your evaluation on proven knowledge instead of beliefs. Let the Market Opportunity Navigator be a mirror in your face, rather than mirroring your own subjective opinion!

Debate as much as you can

One main value of using the structure that the Market Opportunity Navigator provides is to clearly put your thoughts and considerations on the table, and to debate them with others. Use the framework and the language it provides to discuss your analysis with peers and stakeholders. It will enrich your reasoning and will help you to avoid any biases that may tilt your analysis in a wrong direction.

? FAQs

The technology that we are developing is quite specific for the product that we have in mind. Will the Market Opportunity Navigator be relevant for us?

Of course, some technologies or capabilities are more fungible than others. They can more easily be applied to serve different applications and market domains. Yet, almost any technology can be de-linked from its current product and be characterised 'in its own right' to understand its generic functionalities. The Market Opportunity Navigator will help you discover new market opportunities and will make sure that your firm will not get locked in and lose its agility.

There are so many things to do in a start-up and so little time. Why should we take the time to invest in this process?

Indeed, time is one of the scarcest resources for entrepreneurs. We know that. However, because it is so rare, it should be spent wisely. Our natural tendency is to invest our time in troubleshooting and short-term problems. Yet, this approach will likely take us nowhere in the long term. Your choice of market opportunity is one of the most important decisions you will ever make. Take the time to think widely and comprehensively about your options before you commit to a specific path. Make sure that the choice is smart, so that you will not regret it when it's too late. You should also keep in mind the 'learning curve' in applying the Navigator. A significant investment is usually required when you begin working with the Navigator but, over time, you will be able to use it and benefit from it with much less effort.

The common assumption among entrepreneurs and investors is that start-ups must adopt a 'laser-sharp focus' approach, because their resources are scarce. How does it fit your Agile Focus approach?

We have done comprehensive research, involving hundreds of firms, to understand this question. Our studies clearly show that a laser-sharp focus on one narrow path doesn't pay off for most firms! On the contrary: firms that implemented a wider approach – by consciously keeping related market options open – outperformed those who didn't, mainly because of their greater agility. Laser-sharp focus therefore comes at the price of flexibility, while Agile Focus helps you manage the delicate balance between staying focused and staying flexible!

2

The Market Opportunity Navigator:
Three steps for discovering your most valuable
market opportunities

Working with the Market Opportunity Navigator

The Market Opportunity Navigator is carefully designed to turn a complex decision making process into a clear and easy-to-manage task.

It contains one primary design board and three dedicated worksheets.

The Navigator's main design board includes the three parts that are essential for setting a smart market opportunity strategy:

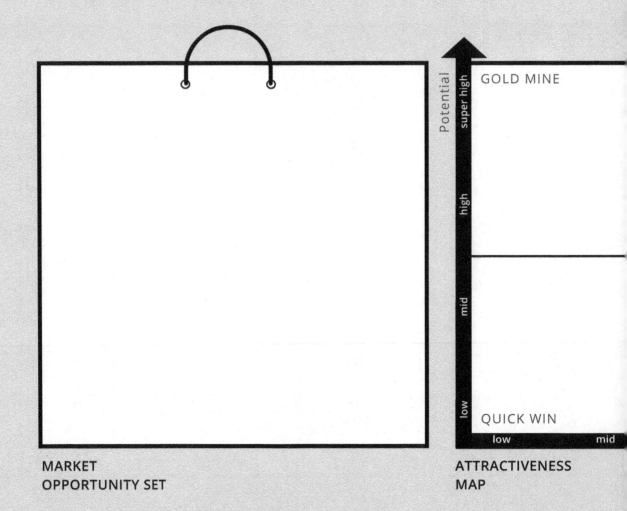

**MARKET
OPPORTUNITY SET**

**ATTRACTIVENESS
MAP**

Use sticky notes to represent each of the market opportunities that you are considering. Place them on the Navigator to display: your Market Opportunity Set, your Attractiveness Map and your Agile Focus Dartboard.

MOON SHOT

PLACE IN STORAGE

KEEP OPEN

PURSUE NOW

QUESTIONABLE

high   super high

Challenge

**AGILE FOCUS
DARTBOARD**

Three worksheets facilitate the achievement of these three key outcomes:

WORKSHEET 1
Generate your Market Opportunity Set

Discover how to describe your core abilities – independent of any (envisioned) product, and how to identify different applications that can be developed with these abilities, along with potential customers who may need these applications. The desired outcome is your Market Opportunity Set.

WORKSHEET 2
Evaluate Market Opportunity Attractiveness

Discover how to rate each option based on two main dimensions – the Potential of the opportunity and the Challenge in capturing its value. The result of this scoring process is depicted in the Attractiveness Map.

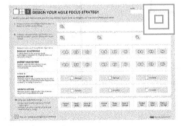

WORKSHEET 3
Design your Agile Focus Strategy

Discover how to assess possible Backup and Growth Options, once the Primary Market Opportunity is chosen. By examining their value and relatedness, you are able to decide which opportunities to pursue now, which will be kept open for later, and which will be placed in storage. The resulting strategy (the 'Agile Focus Strategy') is depicted on the Agile Focus Dartboard.

Once you have gone through the worksheets, you have reached the most important milestone: the complete Market Opportunity Navigator for determining your most promising path.

Remember that both the process and the outcome that the Navigator offers are valuable and important. They will help you to reflect on your learning, communicate your thoughts and determine your strategy.

You are now ready to dive into the inner workings of the Market Opportunity Navigator. We will guide you step by step . . . Enjoy!

Yet, before we begin . . .
Meet Saar and Gal – Founders of Augury.

Saar and Gal are two good friends who always wanted to found a start-up. One day back in 2011, Gal – a software engineer – was sent to India by his employer to diagnose a machine that didn't work properly. He had to fly thousands of miles for that, but as he entered the room he simply heard – with a clear sound – that the problem was not the software, but rather a mechanical malfunction. It was at this moment that an idea came into his mind: why can't we develop something that will simply listen to machines, to diagnose their problems?

A quick technological investigation revealed that developing this technology would be difficult, yet doable. But as they started working on this project, Saar and Gal quickly realised that machines are literally all around us – all the way from complicated manufacturing lines to simple home appliances. So how can they know what type of machines they should 'listen to'? And which market opportunities they should focus on?

As we progress along the three steps of the Market Opportunity Navigator, we will accompany Gal and Saar in their initial market opportunity decision.

2.1 Market Opportunity Set

Your resources and capabilities are typically fungible – this means, they can be used to create products or services not just for customers in one market domain, but for different customers across many market domains. They can be 'leveraged' to create multiple market opportunities for you.

Market Opportunity
We define a market opportunity as the combination of an application of your abilities for a specific set of customers.

Discovering multiple market opportunities is very important for you, because not all market opportunities are alike. Some have greater growth potential, whereas others face much less competition, and again others are just markets that one should avoid as they are difficult and costly to enter. Hence, finding a great market opportunity to exploit is a real advantage, as it can provide you with the fertile ground for growing your business and for reaping the greatest value from your innovation! Don't waste your time with possibly inferior opportunities. Look before you leap!

Additionally, and just as important, once you have identified multiple opportunities, you have a portfolio at hand that offers additional growth possibilities, or the ability to pivot to another market should it become necessary. You can thus unleash the power of multiple opportunities to enhance your agility and manoeuvrability.

> *A Market Opportunity Set is a true asset for your firm!*

In this chapter, we show you how you can identify manifold market opportunities, some closer to what you may have had already in mind, and some far afield. Worksheet 1 will guide you through this process. The result will be your **Market Opportunity Set** that will create much needed strategic choice on your path to commercial success.

Your main takeaways

Identifying potential market opportunities is not an easy task. It requires questioning, observing, experimenting and networking, to understand different customer needs and how you can address them.° Worksheet 1 helps you to generate possible market opportunities, as you adopt these four behaviours. It will help you to think about your own resources and capabilities in a more fungible way, detached from the products that you may have already envisioned, and regardless of whether you have already developed these capabilities or just about to do so.

Ultimately, this structured thinking process opens your mind to different applications that can address different needs of different customers. It actually enhances your *cognitive flexibility*, so you can be more alert to other promising opportunities.

The result is just as important as the process. Having options at hand not only gives you the power of choosing but also the power of staying agile. Remember that options are a real asset for your venture, if you know how to leverage them smartly. Hence: one of the main takeaways from this step is that you leave some long held assumptions (such as 'this is already the perfect market for me') behind, verify your beliefs, and explore what else may be in store for you. You will not regret this later.

Q Research insights

A research study of over 80 venture-capital backed technology start-ups examined the contribution of having multiple market opportunities at hand prior to the firm's first market entry.
The results offered two valuable insights regarding this important early stage in new firm creation:
First, they revealed that one key element that serial entrepreneurs have learned through prior start-up experience is to generate a choice set of market opportunities before deciding which market opportunity to pursue initially.
Second, the analysis clearly showed that entrepreneurs can derive key performance benefits from the identification of a choice set of market opportunities.°°

To find out more take a look at:
o The Innovator's DNA/ Dyer, Gregersen & Christensen (2011)
oo Look before you leap: Market opportunity identification in emerging technology firms'/ Gruber, MacMillan & Thompson (2008)

WORKSHEET 1:
Generating your Market Opportunity Set

Worksheet 1 will assist you in generating a set of market opportunities. It consists of two straightforward steps:

First, think about your unique abilities or core technological elements – independent of their application in a specific product. In particular, list what these elements can accomplish (their functions) and their main properties.

Second, seek out different possible applications that these technological elements can establish, either by combining the elements you listed in different ways or by adding additional technologies to them. Along these lines, think about who may need these different applications. You can further segment these customer sets to identify even more opportunities!

The identified set of market opportunities will then be subject to an evaluation in the following step.

1

GENERATE YOUR MARKET OPPORTUNITY SET

List the venture's core abilities or technological elements.

Characterise them based on their functions and properties. Describe them in a general manner, independent of your (envisioned) product.

ABILITIES

Identify your market opportunities.

Which applications can you offer with your core abilities?
Which customers may need them? Zoom in to further segment each customer group.

APPLICATIONS

CUSTOMERS

application + customer = market opportunity

Place the market opportunities that you would like to evaluate in the Market Opportunity Set.

Step 1: Unique abilities and technologies

The whole process starts with getting a good understanding of your unique abilities or your core technology (or technologies, in case you develop multiple ones). Because your unique abilities form the basis from which you will identify your market opportunities, it is of fundamental importance to understand what they can do – what properties they have and what functions they can perform.

> *When we talk about abilities and technologies, we mean a set of resources and capabilities that you currently have, and also those that you are currently developing or planning to develop.*

Decoupling abilities and use context!

To get to a good understanding of what you can potentially do with your abilities, you will need to think about them 'in their own right'. Imagine them in a more general way, that is, decoupled from the specific product idea or customer need that you may originally have had in mind.

In the upper part of **Worksheet 1** you note the key elements that in combination form your technology or unique abilities. For instance, unique abilities can be an important know-how that you or your venture possesses about a specific process, a rare resource that you have developed, or a special capability (such as manufacturing). Technologies can be 'broken down' into core elements based on their unique functionality (such as pattern recognition, for example), or based on their structural design (such as a nano-sized camera).

Typically, some of these elements and abilities are more generic and some are more specific in nature, i.e., they are there because of the particular functionality that is needed for the specific product you may have in mind. **We urge you to think about and describe your technological elements and abilities in the most generic manner, as they will form the basis for different applications!**

Once done with noting the key technological elements and abilities, briefly describe their main properties as well as the functions they can perform. This description will be an important help for you when searching for new market opportunities!

Augury's technology records ultrasonic sounds and vibrations, with a hardware device called the 'Auguscope'. An algorithm then compares the recording of a specific machine to previous recordings of that same machine as well as recordings of other, similar machines stored on the company's servers. They then display the diagnosis and treatment recommendation to the user. A well-designed user interface allows users to operate the system and tailor its reports from a mobile and a web application.

Regardless of the type of machine they can 'listen to', and the customers who may need it, Saar and Gal – the two founders of Augury – can therefore describe three unique technological elements:

1. They will have a hardware device, which will record the sounds of a machine. This hardware device will include both vibration and ultrasonic sensors, it will be small and portable, and it will operate at a high sampling rate.

2. Augury will develop the 'brains' of their platform – the algorithm that can diagnose a machine's health in mere seconds. This algorithm will be able to compare new and existing data from similar machines in order to detect any changes in real time. It will be designed to work with big data, as the sounds will be recorded and saved on the firm's servers. Adopting a machine learning approach, the algorithm can become stronger and smarter over time, and also develop a malfunction dictionary as it gathers more and more information.

3. Augury's team will develop an easy-to-apply user interface system. This system will allow its users to operate the hardware from any mobile device, and to manage and tailor its output from a mobile and from a web platform.

Here is how these three technological elements should be listed and characterised in the upper part of Worksheet 1:

 Listening Hardware

Records vibrations and ultrasonics

Small

Portable and robust

High sampling rate

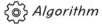 **Algorithm**

Detects changes

Real time analysis

Designed for big data

Based on machine learning

Builds malfunction dictionary

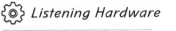 **User Interface**

Easy and intuitive

Suits iPhone and Android platforms

Generates tailored reports and statistics

Online management platform

Unique abilities, however, are not necessarily only technological, as the case of Biotia points out. Biotia is a NY-based start-up that was founded by Niamh – a recent PhD graduate in the field of genomics. Niamh possesses several unique know-hows in this area, including the ability to design effective experiments, to sample complex natural environments, and to monitor all types of pathogens using next-generation DNA sequencing. She decided to found a start-up that can offer environmental surveillance solutions using the power of genomics. Here is how the upper part of Worksheet 1 looks for Biotia:

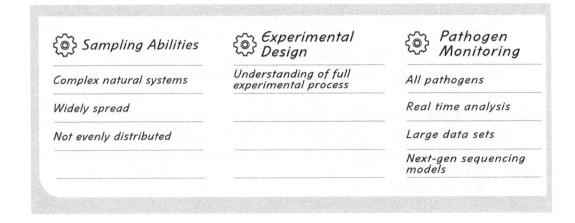

Sampling Abilities

Complex natural systems

Widely spread

Not evenly distributed

Experimental Design

Understanding of full experimental process

Pathogen Monitoring

All pathogens

Real time analysis

Large data sets

Next-gen sequencing models

This step is extremely important not only because it helps you understand what exactly your unique technologies and abilities are but also because it helps in developing your *cognitive flexibility* – the mental ability to develop a variety of viewpoints.

As a result, it will be easier for you to discover other potential applications for your core technologies and abilities – as a whole set, and for each technology and ability by itself, thereby broadening your perspective on what you may currently believe to be just a feature of your (envisioned) product. And this could be of great importance, as the properties or functionalities of such a feature may turn out to be extremely valuable for other applications and markets.

Think about Flickr. This well-known photo-sharing firm started out (as Ludicorp) in 2002 by developing a multiplayer online game with real time interaction through instant messaging. One feature of this game was a chat environment with photo sharing – which quickly became valuable in its own right and surpassed the game itself in popularity, leading the firm to put the game on hold, and to focus on developing a new photo-sharing community site.°

Another example that emphasises the importance of viewing 'features' in their own right, from the outset, is Medic Vision Imaging Solutions. This start-up aimed to develop computer-aided diagnostic tools for brain scans (CTs), to help radiologists in their complicated job. One technological feature which they had to develop for that product was a 'noise reduction' algorithm to improve the quality of the CT before the automatic analysis begins. It took them quite a while to understand that this feature – in its own right – is extremely valuable as it provides the ability to generate high-quality CT images with lower doses of radiation. This understanding led them to shift their strategy and develop the SafeCT, an add-on iterative image reconstruction for low-dose CT imaging. While Medic Vision succeeded in this strategic shift, it was definitely difficult, as they had to put aside years of R&D, find new investors and even change their top management team. A structured analysis of their key features and the opportunities they offer might have saved them from this painful shift along the way, or at least might have helped them to build their venture in a way that would make such pivoting less challenging.

° To find out more take a look at: Founders at Work/ Jessica Livingston (2008)

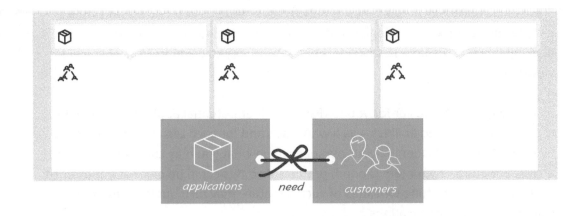

Step 2: Applications and customers: discovering new market opportunities

The discovery of new market opportunities will create your Market Opportunity Set.
A **market opportunity** is any **combination of applications and customers**.
Hence, the discovery process encourages you to think broadly on both ends:
the possible applications and the possible customers. The link that ties both ends is the need: applications are designed to address specific needs of specific customers.

Out of the box: think BROAD

The bottom half of your **Worksheet 1** is dedicated to this DISCOVERY process.
For some, this may be an easy task, but for many this presents a key challenge. The challenge lies not only in uncovering new applications and customers but also in leaving some long held assumptions behind (such as 'this is the already perfect market for me') and explore what else may be in store for you. You will never know unless you look!

BE OPEN, THINK UNCONSTRAINED, SHOW YOUR CREATIVITY – and all of that in a playful manner. The idea is really to get out of your own box and look for market opportunities that could, in fact, be quite distant to the market that you may have thus far envisioned. Essentially, try to generate a wide variety of new opportunities in your discovery process.

> *Take your time,*
> *this is a very important step for your venture or innovation project!*

The example of PayPal's early days, which were described by its co-founder Max Levchin in the book 'Founders at Work', emphasises the importance of thinking broadly about possible applications and customers.

The founders initially developed library codes that allowed users to secure anything on their handheld device. But this unique ability still needed to find its 'killer' application, as Max described: 'Then we started experimenting with the question: what can we store inside the PalmPilot that is actually meaningful?' They thought about enterprise applications (for secured data) and consumer applications (like storing passwords), until finally 'we hit on this idea of why don't we just store money in the handheld devices'.

Indeed, the PayPal founders invested significant effort in finding potential customers with one broad application in mind: securing data on handheld devices. What they had missed, however, is that they could also use their unique abilities to secure data on the web – which could open up other promising opportunities. In fact, they were so hooked on handheld devices that they didn't even notice when users were practically begging for a web application, as Max described: 'Then all these people from a site called eBay were contacting us and saying, "Can I put your logo in my auction?" and we were like: "Why?", so we told them, "No. Don't do it." So for a while we were fighting, tooth and nail, crazy eBay people: "Go away, we don't want you." Eventually we realized that these guys were begging to be our users. We had a moment of epiphany, and for the next 12 months just iterated like crazy on the website version of the product, which is today's PayPal.' Despite this initial, rigid thinking, PayPal managed to adapt – later rather than sooner – and, ultimately, accomplished an immense success!o

The identification challenge

For some technologies it is easier to identify a large and varied set of market opportunities than for others. Consider NanoAF, a start-up that develops a novel coating that prevents bacterial adhesion to surfaces. This coating can be applied on all surfaces (including glass, titanium, metals and polymers). Evidently, this technology can be useful in a large variety of domains, including water treatment, medical devices, marine antifouling, food packaging and air quality control – to name but a few. Because NanoAF's abilities are so general from the outset, identifying a wide variety of market domains is not a very difficult task.

---

o To find out more take a look at: Founders at Work/ Jessica Livingston (2008)

However, even if you develop a more contextualised (specific) technology, you can still search widely to create a large and varied set of options. Inka Robotics is one such example. This start-up developed an autonomous tattooing robot controlled by computer vision and aims to change the tattoo world by revolutionising technology, prices, hygiene and safety. A broad search for additional market opportunities revealed that this robotic machine can also be applied in different medical applications, as well as for computer controlled cutting machines (CNC).

Look for proven tips on how to boost your discovery skills below!

Possible applications

Once you have listed your core abilities and technological elements, it's time to think about them creatively, perhaps recombine them in different possible manners, in order to identify possible applications. An application means a specific usage or function, which you can create with your core technologies and abilities. It can be based on some or all of the key elements you noted in the upper part of Worksheet 1.

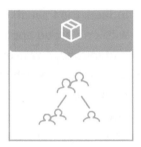

As an example, think about Google Glass – the smart eyewear developed by Google X Labs. This wearable computer had several unique technological elements, including eye-tap technology, voice control, smart prism projector and augmented reality abilities.

This device, which became a catalyst for a huge surge in wearable tech back in 2012, was officially pulled from the market in early 2015. One main reason was that it had been released for consumers without a solidified purpose in mind. Yet, the unique abilities of the Google Glass could actually serve many different applications, other than consumers. It could be used for medical purposes, for educational purposes or for media applications, to name just a few.

Note that you can describe an application in a manner that is detached from any specific customers (e.g., 'environmental monitoring') or in a way that already signals specific users or the broad market domain (e.g., 'medical device').

Combining your technology with other technologies

Another powerful way to jump-start your imagination when identifying new applications is to think about combining your technology with others . . . and thereby add functionality – which, in turn, may broaden the appeal of your technology to new customer sets.

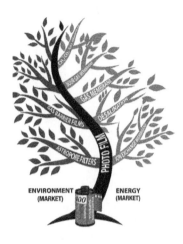

Fujifilm is an interesting example for such combinations. Originally, Fujifilm brought photographic film production to Japan and grew based on this business. By researching and developing for many decades everything related to photographic film, from raw materials to processes to systems, Fujifilm became an expert in many different advanced materials technologies, including coatings, membranes and organic compounds. By combining these abilities with newly developed technologies, the company today creates unique materials that can be used in an extremely wide variety of applications, including desalination, gas membranes and AstroPore filters. In fact, the company's website presents the tree shown here, to emphasise how core technologies can be leveraged to create different products in multiple domains, far beyond its original market.°

Possible customers

Applications are designed to address specific needs. Hence, as you uncover potential applications, you should also consider who may have the need for them. These will create your possible sets of customers.

Think as broadly as possible about who may have the need for your applications. For example, environmental monitoring could be useful for hospitals, for child-care institutes and for food manufacturers, to name a few.

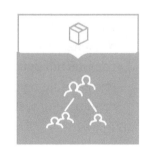

Use the bottom half of Worksheet 1 to list your possible applications and customers. This will help you see new market opportunities.

Here is what it looks like for Augury:

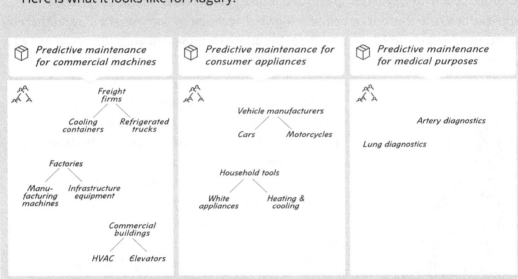

Augury's technology can be applied to offer predictive maintenance for commercial machines, for consumer appliances and for medical purposes. Each of these applications already alludes to a fairly general market domain.

Next, in the customers' section, different market segments can be listed for each application. For instance, commercial machines include customer segments such as factories, commercial buildings and freight firms.

Each of these groups requires further segmentation to arrive at the largest homogenous customer set. For example, as Gal and Saar zoomed into commercial buildings, they understood that their offer could be relevant for maintaining elevators, or for maintaining heating, ventilation and air conditioning systems (HVAC).

Zoom in and zoom out on possible customers

Identifying a set of customers for an application is in many cases just the beginning of your discovery process. Zoom in on potential customer segments to identify sub-segments (e.g., further investigations by Augury's team revealed that the HVAC market for commercial buildings could be additionally segmented into service providers or building-management companies). Or zoom out to identify a broader set of users that may open your mind to other segments (e.g., zooming out of the commercial building market can lead to maintenance opportunities in residential buildings).

Let's look at ForNova to better understand the zooming-in process in customer discovery. This start-up develops visual scanning software that mimics human behaviour and 'reads' content like pricing, images, descriptions and ratings. As such, it can gather on-line data that isn't hindered by changes in code, language or layout.

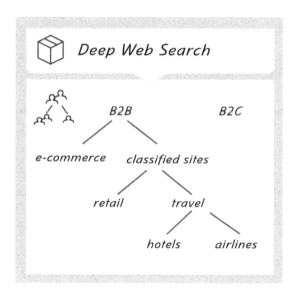

In Worksheet 1, their customer tree begins with understanding whether they will serve consumers (B2C) or businesses (B2B). Zooming into the B2B domain, they could serve e-commerce firms or classified sites. Within the classified market domain, they could focus on the travel market or the retail market, and zooming-in further shows how the travel market can be broken down into hotels and airlines. In sum, this zooming-in process helps in identifying a wider range of potential customers and in understanding how to group them properly.

Continents and countries

The zooming-in activity encourages you to further segment a broad market domain into more concrete groups of users, thereby creating different possible levels of analysis.

You can also think about this as the 'continents vs. countries' issue in market opportunity identification: a continent, for this matter, is a broad market domain (or a vertical). And every continent contains multiple countries – or market segments. In order to arrive at a consistent Market Opportunity Set, you will need to have opportunities that are on the same level of abstraction. Otherwise, it will be very difficult to compare them with each other.

For instance, in the ForNova example, you can think about the evaluation of the e-commerce market domain relative to classified sites as a 'continent' level of analysis, whereas retail and travel can be viewed as 'countries' within one continent. Of course, it is possible to compare countries from different continents, yet it would be misleading when you compare countries to continents – as they represent different levels of analysis.

The goal is to arrive at a level of abstraction that you feel comfortable with during your evaluation (which is the next step of the Navigator). Too broad is not good, as it will become difficult to truly compare market opportunities with each other. In fact, in a fairly broad market domain there are likely some segments that will provide you with more fertile ground for your efforts than others! Too narrow is often not good either, as you will want a market opportunity that addresses a homogeneous customer set that is still sufficiently large to warrant your efforts!

Back to Augury . . .

As the Augury example shows, it may sometimes be necessary to start by comparing different continents, even though they average many types of countries. Gal and Saar understood that when they discovered that their diagnostic technology could be suitable not only for industrial machines but also for the human body – a complex machine in its own right! The decision whether Augury should diagnose machines or bodies is a continent analysis, and a critical one to begin with, because it is almost impossible to move from one domain to another given the heavy investments and the unique know-how and reputation that each of these domains requires.

To make this major decision, Gal and Saar had to understand first the possible different market segments within each continent and then had to evaluate the overall potential and challenges in each continent (as we will discuss in detail in the following chapter). Overall, they discovered that their offering could be disruptive in machine maintenance (as they could turn to a market that historically lacked the ability to perform predictive maintenance), while many big players are already attempting to offer predictive healthcare products in the medical domain. Hence, they considered the potential of the machine domain to be higher, and the overall challenge to be a bit lower – because medical devices require heavy regulation.

Thus, Augury's founders chose to focus on predictive maintenance for machines and to put aside the medical market.

In sum: This discovery process is extremely important. Be open and discover as many, and as varied, market opportunities as you possibly can! Having 3–5 market opportunities in your Market Opportunity Set is typically a good starting point. We have worked with start-ups that could identify more than 50 market opportunities before they performed an initial screening. So, don't give up too early.

Turbo boost your discovery skills

Over the past 15 years, we have met with a large number of entrepreneurs and innovators, and also engaged in large-scale research on the secrets of those who have 'superior vision' of the market opportunity landscape.[o] Here are some powerful tactics that you can use to boost your own discovery skills:

Mine your knowledge

People will primarily discover market opportunities that are associated with their own existing knowledge of customer problems. It is easy: you will most likely see those opportunities that relate to your prior knowledge! But typically you only invoke parts of that knowledge . . . so: take your time, and try to remember all the instances in which you came across people (or firms) experiencing a problem that could be solved with the functionality inherent in your technology! But don't be too strict with yourself . . . having a hunch about a potential customer problem is a good start for more systematic investigations.

Access external sources

Because people tend to see market opportunities that are related to their existing knowledge, and are blind to others, one straightforward way to increase your vision of the market opportunity landscape is to open up your search to include others – for instance, this can be other people in your team, friends from different industries, or you could use one of the crowd search platforms on the web. Independent of the way, make sure that you describe the functionalities of your technology very well, and in layman terms, so that others do understand what your technology can do!

Ploughing lists of industries and markets

In order to systematically jump-start your creativity, or simply to help your memory, you can also consult existing lists of industries and markets. Often, these are hierarchically ordered, so that you can easily zoom in and zoom out of domains and consider whether your technology may be useful to customers in that domain!

Perform a patent search

Whenever relevant, you can search for patents that are closely related to or form the basis for the technology you are planning to develop. This could give you some ideas in which industries and by which companies similar technologies were applied.

---

[o] To find out more take a look at: Escaping the prior knowledge corridor: What shapes the number and variety of market opportunities identified before market entry of technology start-ups?/ Gruber, MacMillan & Thompson (2012)

Initial screening of your options

Once you have discovered multiple options, you may want to do an initial screening with some limited research in order to weed out those that are not sufficiently promising or that have some fatal flaws. In fact, having such 'no-goes' at this stage is quite natural, as it is a sign that you searched broadly and creatively for new ideas – and some may just not be what they originally seemed to be!

Key questions you can ask for an initial screening are:

▢ Does the customer need exist?

▢ Can we really satisfy the customer need using our unique abilities, and better than existing solutions?

▢ Are there severe restrictions that would hinder us from executing on this market opportunity?

▢ Will this opportunity be in conflict with any of our core values?

Once you are done with this initial screening you either may want to go back to another round of market discovery or, if you are happy with the outcome (i.e., you have several market opportunities in your set which you want to further consider), you have arrived at our first key result!

The outcome – your Market Opportunity Set

You are now ready to depict your Market Opportunity Set on the Navigator's main design board. Make sure that you give each market opportunity a clear name.

Use sticky notes to represent each of the market opportunities in your set, and place them in the designated area.

> *And remember, these could all turn out to be important value creation and growth opportunities for you.*

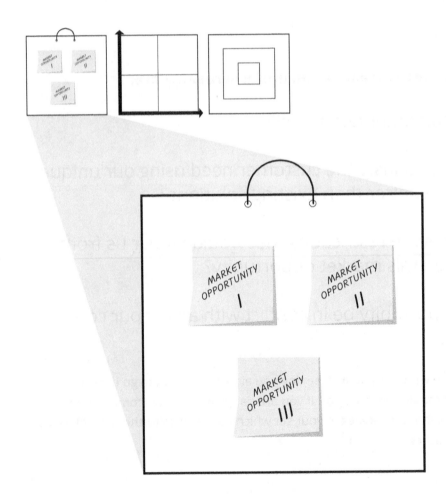

It's time for Augury to define their Market Opportunity Set.

Augury's team discovered many potential market opportunities. In an initial and rough screening process, they decided to further examine five markets that seemed most interesting: HVAC for commercial buildings, manufacturing lines in factories, cooling containers for freight companies, cars' and white appliances' manufacturers.

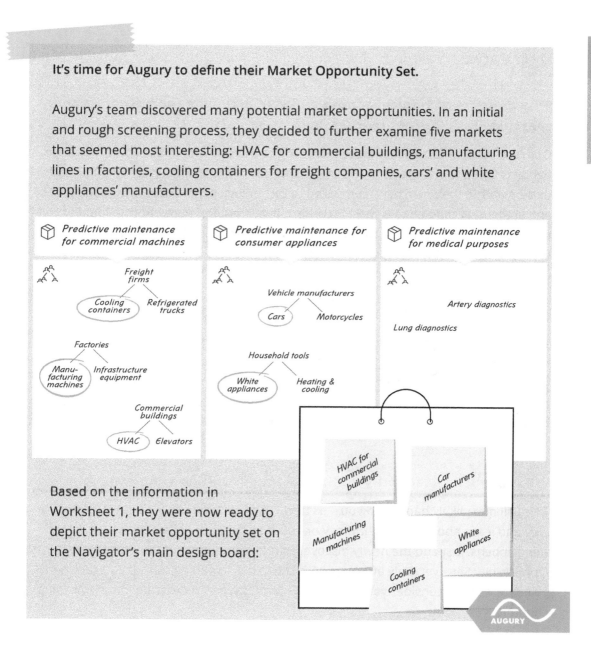

Based on the information in Worksheet 1, they were now ready to depict their market opportunity set on the Navigator's main design board:

Remember that this is a dynamic process. You can add opportunities to your set over time, if you uncover new options that require your attention, or you can discard options from your set, if you find that these are not worthy enough.

? FAQs

Why do some technologies pose a bigger challenge than others when searching for different market opportunities?

Our research has shown that those technologies that are more abstract and that are tightly coupled with a specific application context are more difficult to decouple and understand 'in their own right' compared to technologies that address human senses and are loosely coupled to a specific context. It will require more effort to identify market opportunities for the former, and it will also require strong technological expertise to do so.°

When should I stop searching and start my evaluation?

You may keep on searching and searching and keep on discovering ever new market opportunities along the way. Yet, at some point you will need to stop, as your ultimate goal is to commercialise your innovation. From our research we know that there are also decreasing returns to search, that means, after a while you have identified your main market opportunities. Shoot for 3–5 market opportunities in your set!

What happens if I identify additional opportunities as I move along?

This will most likely happen to you – as new customers may approach you along the way and learn about your technology or you may simply have a new insight. When this happens, just add the newly discovered market opportunity to your Market Opportunity Set – yet, only after it passes the initial screening round! You can then evaluate it and reconsider your Agile Focus Strategy, as we describe in the following chapter.

° To find out more take a look at: The micro-foundations of technology leveraging across markets/ Gruber & Thiel (working paper)

GOLD MINE

MOON SHOT

QUICK WIN

QUESTIONABLE

2.2 Attractiveness Map

A set of potential market opportunities is a valuable asset for your business. However, as in all situations in life where you have to make a choice they are likely to create a dilemma for you: which option is your primary opportunity – the one which you will pursue with full force? And which ones do you put aside for now?

To make this important decision, you will first have to evaluate your options, as opportunities differ in their level of attractiveness. This is exactly what this stage is all about: an attractive market opportunity is one that will likely produce significant **potential** for value creation and that poses relatively few **challenges** in capturing that value!

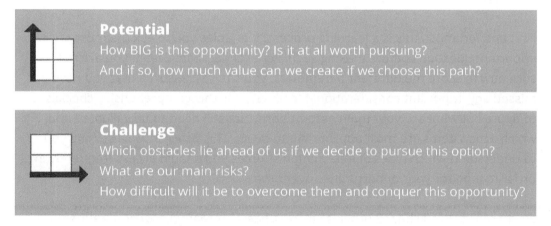

Potential
How BIG is this opportunity? Is it at all worth pursuing?
And if so, how much value can we create if we choose this path?

Challenge
Which obstacles lie ahead of us if we decide to pursue this option?
What are our main risks?
How difficult will it be to overcome them and conquer this opportunity?

In this chapter we show you how you can evaluate the **Potential** and the **Challenge** inherent in your market opportunities, using Worksheet 2.

Once you have rated each opportunity on these two dimensions, you can place it on the **Attractiveness Map**. This map is your guide to understand the very nature of each individual opportunity and your whole set of opportunities. It thus helps you to better grasp the trade-offs existing among opportunities, to compare them and to reveal your most attractive options. Ultimately, the Attractiveness Map is your tool to make an informed choice of your Primary Market Opportunity – a choice that takes into account the most important data points and that will not be based mostly on intuition (which often suffers from one's own biases).

Moreover, the Attractiveness Map is a dynamic tool which helps you to reflect on any new information that becomes available – as you can easily update the Potential or the Challenge associated with your opportunities and relocate your options if necessary, or simply add new ones.

Your main takeaways

Worksheet 2 guides you on how to evaluate your set of market opportunities. The outcome of this task – the scoring of your options – has great value for any business owner who wants to choose smartly which market opportunities to play in. Yet, the process in and of itself is beneficial as well.

First and foremost, this is a learning process. It enables you to ask the most important questions before making such a critical decision. Even if you are not sure how to score the different parameters, you can rest assured that you have not missed any important consideration. Moreover, use this comprehensive checklist to figure out what are your main assumptions that still need to be validated and which action items are most appropriate to do so. This process will also help you to understand which types of information sources you should access frequently in order to monitor your opportunities over time.

Furthermore, Worksheet 2 provides a great basis for team discussion – either with your peers or with your stakeholders. These discussions bring different perspectives to the table and will facilitate your understanding. Eventually, you will get a better sense of your alternatives and become more sensitive to the upsides and downsides of each market opportunity.

Lastly, the Attractiveness Map that will be derived from Worksheet 2 provides you with the 'big picture' that allows you to better understand the relative assessment of your options from a bird's eye perspective. The ability to drill down and see the big picture at the same time is of key importance for making a smart decision.

It's a learning process!

The evaluation that you will perform for each option is one of the most important learning processes in entrepreneurship and innovation. Take time to research and study, and to gather all the knowledge you can before you make the fundamental decision about which market(s) to enter with your company.

In short, adopt a learning mindset:

Be systematic

The structure of the evaluation process makes sure that you will not overlook key issues. It helps you to be consistent throughout, so that you can compare your options based on the same set of considerations.

Turn hypotheses into knowledge

A learning process usually starts with hypotheses or beliefs that you have about the opportunity that you want to analyse. Yet, a valid evaluation should not be based on beliefs: try to turn your critical assumptions into knowledge as you progress through the evaluation and the scoring process. Perform desk research and make sure to 'go out of the building' and talk with customers and market experts. If feasible, conduct some small experiments with customers, as methods such as design thinking and lean start-up suggest.○

Get used to uncertainty

Uncertainty is normal when bringing innovation to the marketplace. Hence, there are also limits to your evaluation. As systematic and thorough as you may want to be, there is still not a crystal ball that can tell you the future: 'known-unknowns' as well as 'unknown-unknowns' can both influence the validity of your scoring. Yet, don't let this fogginess stop you from performing your evaluation. Try gathering the most critical information and validate it as much as you can before making a decision. And just as important: update your evaluation once new data becomes available. This is exactly why the Market Opportunity Navigator is designed to be a companion for your innovation journey – a dynamic tool that helps you navigate over time!

○ To find out more take a look at: The Lean Startup/ Eric Ries (2011); The Four Steps to the Epiphany/ Steve Blank (2005); Design Thinking/ Thomas Lockwood (2009)

Before starting your evaluation

Preparation can go a long way when striving for success. So, there's some homework to accomplish before you can get to the actual scoring of your options based on their Potential and their Challenge. Learn about and understand (1) your customers' world, (2) the business environment and (3) the key milestones on the road to implementation.

Learn about your customers' world

'If you're going to be good at fishing, you've got to learn to think like a fish.' Putting yourself in the shoes of your customers is critical for understanding the essence of your market opportunity. What is the value proposition that you bring to your customers? What pain are you addressing and why is your offer better than current solutions? What do these customers value, and what important trends influence them? Without a clear understanding of these questions, your evaluation will be of limited value.[o]

Learn about your business environment

You will not compete in a vacuum. Because many other players could influence your chances of success, you need to understand your playground very well. To be able to evaluate a market opportunity, you'll need to understand the **value chain** of this market (i.e., the string of companies or players that work together to satisfy the market demand for a given product). Where will you fit in? Who could stand in your way? And who has an incentive to collaborate with you? In fact, innovative ideas often break existing value chains and change them completely (e.g., think about Apple iTunes), so a comprehensive understanding of all the relevant players is critical.
In addition, you also need to understand who could be your **competitors** in this market: What do they offer? How would they react? And do you have a strong (perhaps even 'unfair') competitive advantage over them?[oo]

Understand your key milestones on the road to implementation

You will also have to understand your own resources and capabilities: What do you already have, and what do you still need to develop in order to create your product and to deliver it to the market? Think about your technological know-how, human capital, intellectual property, allies and partners, financial resources etc.

To find out more take a look at:
o   Value Proposition Design/ Osterwalder, Pigneur, Bernarda & Smith (2014)
oo Competitive Advantage/ Michael Porter (1985)

Augury's learning process

Saar and Gal took the time to study their market opportunities. They clearly understood the importance of this initial decision and wanted to make sure they had all the necessary information at hand to make the right choice.

They followed key elements of the Lean Start-up approach to test their assumptions on each of their five market opportunities. They performed interviews, showed mockups, handed out some surveys and visited several conferences – to be able to understand the customers' world and the business environment of each option. Gradually, they got to know the ecosystem and the value chain in each market, and to deeply understand the value proposition that they could offer to each actor.

They documented and updated their knowledge on each market, to figure out what should be their next action items for validating the market. This learning process, coupled with a structured set of evaluation criteria – such as the one offered in Worksheet 2 – enabled them to progress from pure intuition to an informed decision.

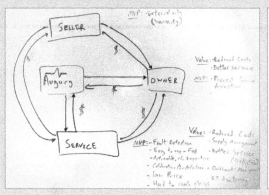
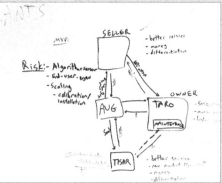

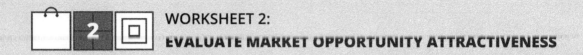

WORKSHEET 2:
EVALUATE MARKET OPPORTUNITY ATTRACTIVENESS

Use this worksheet for every market opportunity you would like to evaluate.

 Market opportunity

POTENTIAL

LOW	MID	HIGH	SUPER HIGH

COMPELLING REASON TO BUY
Unmet need
Effective solution
Better than current solutions

LOW	MID	HIGH	SUPER HIGH

MARKET VOLUME
Current market size
Expected growth

LOW	MID	HIGH	SUPER HIGH

ECONOMIC VIABILITY
Margins (value vs. cost)
Customers' ability to pay
Customer stickiness

OVERALL POTENTIAL

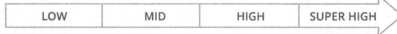

LOW	MID	HIGH	SUPER HIGH

Use the overall ratings to situate each market opportunity on the Attractiveness Map.

CHALLENGE

LOW	MID	HIGH	SUPER HIGH

IMPLEMENTATION OBSTACLES

Product development difficulties

Sales and distribution difficulties

Funding challenges

LOW	MID	HIGH	SUPER HIGH

TIME TO REVENUE

Development time

Time between product and market readiness

Length of sale cycle

LOW	MID	HIGH	SUPER HIGH

EXTERNAL RISKS

Competitive threat

Third party dependencies

Barriers to adoption

OVERALL CHALLENGE

LOW	MID	HIGH	SUPER HIGH

WORSHEET 2
Evaluating Market Opportunity Attractiveness

Worksheet 2 helps you to evaluate each market opportunity along two primary dimensions: **Potential** and **Challenge**.

Each dimension is comprised of three different factors, which are scored separately, and which are then combined to achieve an overall rating for each market opportunity. You will then use this overall rating to place each market opportunity on your Attractiveness Map.

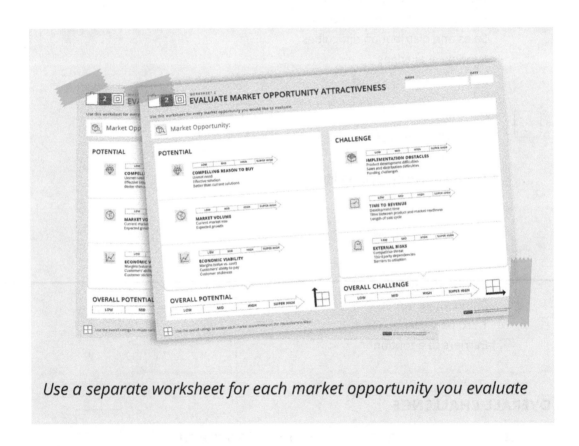

Use a separate worksheet for each market opportunity you evaluate

How to score?

Although it would be easiest if you could derive the overall rating of an opportunity by plugging the scores of each of the six factors into a mathematical formula, such a mechanistic approach would not do justice to the complexities of the underlying decision.

Instead, look at these factors as providing you a comprehensive understanding of the key elements that one should assess when judging the attractiveness of a market opportunity. For each factor that contributes to the Potential or to the Challenge of an opportunity, the following pages give you a list of questions that guide you in this evaluation process. Think thoroughly about these questions and gather all the information that you can, as you score each factor on a scale ranging from 'Low' to 'Super High'. Combine your qualitative and quantitative insights to do that, and strive to be as objective as possible. Team discussions will greatly help here!

Remember that the overall goal is to understand the main upsides and downsides of each option, so don't get too frustrated if you feel that your scoring is not yet 100% accurate! You can also refine your scoring over time, as you learn more about each option separately, and relatively to others.

Overall, scoring the Potential and the Challenge of your opportunities will help you to recognise the patterns and to distinguish between your options . . . so that your most promising strategic path becomes visible!

Potential

The assessment of the Potential of a market opportunity is critical to your evaluation, as it allows you to understand the value that could be created by exploiting this opportunity. In short, how valuable will it be to pursue this option?

This evaluation refers to the opportunity in and of itself, regardless of your own capabilities to succeed in it. (Note: your ability to successfully exploit the market opportunity will be evaluated in the Challenge dimension.)

> *Imagine that the set of possible market opportunities create the landscape in which your venture should travel. If each market opportunity is a mountain on this landscape, this dimension measures the height of the mountain, so that the higher the mountain, the greater the potential value it can offer to you.*

The value creation potential of a market opportunity is shaped by three primary factors:

Compelling reason to buy
Will someone really want our offer and be willing to pay for it?

Market volume
How big is this market, now and in the near future?

Economic viability
Is it worthwhile from a business perspective to pursue this market?

We recommend that you evaluate each factor separately and then combine your scores into the rating of the overall Potential.

Compelling reason to buy

What does it mean?

If no one wants to buy it, it isn't worth anything . . . So the first thing you need to learn about a market opportunity is whether someone will really want what you have to offer. If compelling reason to buy is low – it's simply a 'No-Go', as demand will not fly.

How to evaluate?

Look deeply into three important questions:

Is there a real unmet need?

Can we provide an effective solution to this need?

And can we address it (much) better than current solutions?

An honest answer to these questions can lead you into estimating the strength of your potential customer's reason to buy. Here is a non-exhaustive list of questions that can guide you when searching for answers.

A real unmet need?

☐ What exactly is the problem/ need/ job to be done? Is it functional, social, emotional or basic need?

☐ Who exactly has this need? Try to characterise a common customer. Who will be your economic buyer? Your user?

☐ How do they currently solve the problem? Do they make an effort to actually solve the problem?

☐ What will change with our offer? What are its main benefits? Are they economic, functional, emotional, self-expressive or social? If economic (e.g., increased productivity on key success factors/ reduced costs) – try to estimate the value and the return on investment in actual numbers.

☐ Is it a 'nice to have', 'should have' or a 'must have' offer?

☐ Make vs. buy possibility – can customers make it themselves?

Provide an effective solution?

☐ Can you fully address the needs of these customers and provide them with a whole solution?[o]

☐ Do you create other needs – which you can't address – for the customers that will use your solution?

☐ What strengths do you have that allow you to address this need, or do this job well?

☐ What weaknesses do you have that hinder you from addressing this need?

Better than current solutions?

☐ What other solutions exist for your customers?

☐ What are the upsides of your solution relative to others? Why would customers prefer your product?

☐ What are the downsides of your solution relative to others? Why would customers not prefer your product?

☐ Are the advantages of your solution really meaningful for the customers?

Important to remember

Note that the only way to score this factor is to look through the eyes of your customers. It's not what you think, it's what they think – what they say, or even more importantly, what they do. Validate your beliefs, go out of the building and talk about this market opportunity with as many potential customers as possible. Several books can help you as you design your customers' interviews.[oo]

Once you have thoroughly gone over these questions, you will be able to score your level of 'compelling reason to buy'. If you find it helpful, you can also score each of the sub-elements separately and then combine their grade into an overall score.

LOW	MID	HIGH	SUPER HIGH

To find out more take a look at:
o   Crossing the Chasm/ Geoffrey Moore (1991)
oo The Entrepreneur's Guide to Customer Development/ Cooper & Vlaskovits (2010);
    Running Lean/ Ash Maurya (2010); Talking to Humans/ Giff Constable (2014)

To illustrate the assessment of this factor, let's go back to Augury.
One market opportunity that they thoroughly considered was HVAC systems (heating, ventilation and air conditioning) for commercial buildings. They believed that managers or service providers of large commercial buildings will benefit from predictive maintenance equipment that can monitor all the HVAC systems. Such a product will not only help to eliminate failures but will also extend the operational life of the system and will reduce operational expenses and energy consumption.

To assess the compelling reason to buy of this market they talked with many potential customers and carefully examined alternative solutions. They found that implementing current predictive maintenance solutions requires very high investment, which is disproportional to the cost of an HVAC system breakdown. Augury's solution will be able to offer a relatively cheap solution with no upfront investment. The need for predictive maintenance in this market, thus, clearly exists. However, the customers themselves are not aware of predictive maintenance possibilities, so that Augury will actually need to educate the market in order to create awareness to this unmet need and induce demand.

In terms of effective solution, as HVACs are standardised systems, Augury could develop a product that would address the customer's need in a complete manner, and provide alerts and reports on most types of malfunctions. As no solutions were tailored to this market, their product would also be much better than current predictive maintenance solutions.

Overall, they scored the compelling reason to buy as 'mid-high', especially since customers were not aware of this unmet need.

 Market Opportunity: *HVAC for Commercial Buildings*

LOW	MID	HIGH	SUPER HIGH

COMPELLING REASON TO BUY
Unmet need, Effective solution, Better than current solutions

Market volume

What does it mean?

Satisfying a real need is an important condition for creating value. Yet, it is the market volume that will determine to what extent you can sell your product and, thus, to what extent you will create that potential value!

To understand market volume, you need to estimate how many customers actually face (or are expected to face) this need in the near future and how much they will be willing to pay. The size of the market provides key indications for how BIG this market opportunity is. Although market size is important, a market which is not BIG may still be an interesting option, especially if it can become a stepping stone towards a larger market that can be exploited later on.

How to evaluate?

Look deeply into two main questions:

What is the size of the current market?

How much is it expected to grow over time?

Objective answers to these questions are the basis for estimating the size or volume of the market. Here are some questions that can guide you when searching for these numbers.

Current market size?

▢ How many customers need your solution? You can estimate the total number of potential customers in a bottom-up or a top-down approach, depending on the data that you have.

▢ How many customers can actually use or buy your solution? This is an initial filter to narrow down the 'universe' of all customers. Alternatively, you can think about the TAM (total available market) and the SAM (served available market), as suggested by Steve Blank.°

° To find out more take a look at: The Startup Owner's Manual/ Blank & Dorf (2012)

☐ How many units would these customers buy annually and what would be the annual revenues per customer? Combine the figures to estimate the total market size, that is, how large is the market if they all would buy (in units and in dollars)?

☐ Alternatively, you can estimate the size of the problem, that is, how much do customers spend annually today to deal with the pain you are addressing?

Expected market growth?

☐ Is the market mature or in flux? Has it grown in the last two years?

☐ How much do you expect the need, or the number of customers, to grow in the next 2–5 years?

Important to remember

We recommend to break down the size of the market into two elements: units and dollars. These complementary measures provide a better overview of the expected volume.

Clearly, some markets are more difficult to estimate than others. Steve Blank suggests that there are three main types of markets: existing, re-segmented and new.[o] The first two are easier to gauge, as customers can be more explicit about their needs, and data about the market is often readily available. New markets, however, have no customers, no well-defined competitors and no products yet, so measuring the size of the opportunity is more of a 'guesstimation' than an exact evaluation. In any case, to size a market you will have to talk to people that could be interested in the product and to representatives in the sales channels, look for competitive approximations and search for existing analyst reports and relevant market researches. Google Analytics and Google Trends can also provide initial hints for sizing the demand.

Once you have thoroughly gone over these questions, you will be able to score your 'market volume'. If you find it helpful, you can also score each of the sub-elements separately and then combine their grade into an overall score.

---

[o] To find out more take a look at: The Four Steps to the Epiphany/ Steve Blank (2005)

To illustrate the assessment of this factor, let's look again at the HVAC market for commercial buildings.

There are countless commercial buildings with HVAC systems worldwide. Even if Augury initially limits itself to the US market, there are millions of such buildings (in fact, the Commercial Buildings Energy Consumption Survey shows that there were 5.6 million commercial buildings in the USA in 2012, i.e., the time when Augury investigated the market).

Augury's founders estimated that the annual revenues per building would be around $5000, which overall turns out to create a very large market size, both in units and in dollars.

Research analysts also predict that the global HVAC market will grow steadily in the next few years (at an annual growth rate of around 7%), mainly due to the increase in construction activities worldwide.

Thus, the overall market volume for this opportunity can be scored as 'high'.

 Market Opportunity: *HVAC for Commercial Buildings*

LOW	MID	HIGH	SUPER HIGH

MARKET VOLUME
Current market size
Expected growth

 ## Economic viability

What does it mean?

The last factor for assessing the Potential of a market opportunity estimates the economic benefit of this option for you. Without getting into a detailed sales plan or return-on-investment (ROI) calculations, it refers to the basic elements that influence the economic value of a market opportunity.

How to evaluate

At this early point of evaluation, the creation of a detailed financial plan (with 3–5 years of profit and loss estimations) is typically not feasible as most of the information that flows into such a plan is too vague. Instead, you can get a relatively good understanding of the economic potential of a market opportunity by examining three main questions:

Do you have sizeable margins?

Are the customers well funded to pay the price?

How sticky will customers be?

An objective answer to these questions can get you a long way towards understanding to what extent a market opportunity is economically promising. Here are some questions that will help you when searching for answers.

Margins (value vs. cost)?

- ☐ What is the estimated price that customers will be willing to pay?
- ☐ What is the estimated cost of your product/ service?
- ☐ What is the estimated acquisition cost per customer?
- ☐ What are the expected margins (i.e., the economic potential per customer)?
- ☐ Are they expected to change over time (due to economies of scale, improved availability of components etc.)?

Customers' ability to pay?

☐ Are the customers well funded (in general)?

☐ Do the customers already have a budget to solve the problem you are addressing with your offering (especially relevant in B2B)?

☐ Is there someone who is economically responsible for this budget (especially relevant in B2B)?

Customer stickiness?

☐ How frequently will customers use your solution or rebuy it?

☐ How difficult is it for your customers to switch to alternative solutions?

Important to remember

Economic viability of your opportunity is essential, as it will ultimately allow your venture to survive and grow. While it is challenging to know the future price tag of your offering, it is important to understand – and to make sure – that you have enough slack between the cost of your offer and how much customers are willing to pay for it. In any case, make sure to talk with your 'economic buyers' to understand their perspective. Additionally, try to seek comparable offers, which can serve as a signal for how much you can charge for your offering.

Similar challenges arise when assessing your costs: a rough estimation is probably the best you can do for now, yet it is better than nothing! Remember that costs may decrease over time, as economies of scale may kick in.

Despite the importance of this factor, there are many examples of successful companies that did not have a clear revenue model to begin with, but trusted that growth in customer traction would lead to substantial economic reward (e.g., think about Instagram and Waze). In that case, take into account that your economic viability is highly risky and will only be substantive in the long term.

Once you have thoroughly gone over these questions, you will be able to score the level of 'economic viability'. If you find it helpful, you can also score each of the sub-elements separately and then combine their grade into an overall score.

To illustrate the assessment of this factor, let's look again at the HVAC market for commercial buildings. To estimate the economic viability, it is important to first evaluate the value that customers can derive from Augury's solution. Studies estimate that a properly functioning predictive maintenance programme can provide commercial facilities' savings of approximately $1 per square foot annually, resulting in total savings of up to 13% of their operational budget. These estimations led Augury's founders to conclude that the value vs. price ratio is relatively high.

Moreover, although initial costs will be relatively high, due to development hurdles and low economies of scale, these customers were relatively well funded and could afford a price tag that is significantly greater than these costs. The question of whether customers will stay loyal was difficult to answer. Because their algorithm was based on machine learning, it provides more accurate diagnostics by listening to the same machine over time. This should be an incentive for customers to stick with Augury's solution. However, once competitive offerings will pop up in the market, this switching barrier may not be high enough.

Overall, these considerations resulted in scoring the economic viability of this market opportunity as "high".

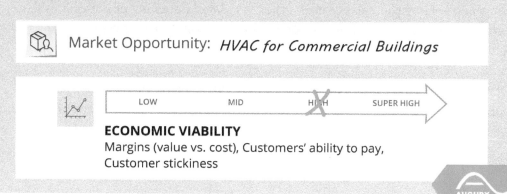

Market Opportunity: *HVAC for Commercial Buildings*

LOW   MID   HIGH   SUPER HIGH

ECONOMIC VIABILITY
Margins (value vs. cost), Customers' ability to pay, Customer stickiness

Potential: the overall rating

Once you have analysed these three key factors, it's time to combine your ratings into an overall score that indicates the Potential of the market opportunity.

Use your individual ratings to arrive at an average score that ranges from 'low' to 'super high'. It will later be used to locate this market opportunity on the Attractiveness Map: the value creation Potential is the Y-axis.

LOW	MID	HIGH	SUPER HIGH

Note that an average score may hide information regarding the key up- or downsides of a market opportunity. However, the important element here is that you have gone through all the major considerations for evaluating the potential of a market opportunity. By now, you know its main advantages and disadvantages, and can keep in mind any major up- or downsides.

Assigning weights to different factors

Are all factors of the same importance?

This is a straightforward question with no straightforward answer.

The value to the customers (the compelling reason to buy) is a necessary condition, and therefore also the first to be analysed. If it is relatively low, it will make your life difficult – independent of any advantages associated with the other factors. However, value and volume can balance each other to create interesting opportunities (e.g., very high value to relatively low volume, or vice versa). The overall picture, thus, really depends on all three factors.

Of course, it is possible to assign different weights to different factors in case the opportunities you are looking at warrant such an approach. But be careful – if you do weigh factors differently, make sure to be consistent across options.

For Augury, the overall Potential of the HVAC opportunity was relatively high. Although they had to educate the market, they believed that the effort was worthwhile since the market was big enough and economically promising.

Market Opportunity: *HVAC for Commercial Buildings*

POTENTIAL

LOW	MID		HIGH	SUPER HIGH

COMPELLING REASON TO BUY
Unmet need
Effective solution
Better than currrent solutions

LOW	MID	HIGH		SUPER HIGH

MARKET VOLUME
Current market size
Expected growth

LOW	MID	HIGH		SUPER HIGH

ECONOMIC VIABILITY
Margins (value vs. cost)
Customers' ability to pay
Customer stickiness

OVERALL POTENTIAL

LOW	MID	HIGH		SUPER HIGH

AUGURY

Sometimes a market opportunity can promise high potential even though the market itself is not very big (in volume). Microbot Medical is one such example. One of the company's products is an autonomous crawling micro-robot that is controlled by electromagnetic fields.

This breakthrough technology is ideal for performing micro-invasive medical procedures in a variety of areas, including neurosurgery, cardiology, gynaecology and many more. One market opportunity that the company considered – and later chose to initially focus on – was self-cleaning shunts for treating the condition of 'water in the brain' (also known as hydrocephalus). Although the market volume for such treatment is not very big (approximately 40,000 procedures for shunt-related surgeries are performed annually in the USA), the value that this product offers is enormous – to the patients and to the insurance companies, so the reimbursement is attractive and there are no other competitive solutions. The compelling reason to buy and the economic viability of this opportunity are therefore 'super high', making this a high potential option.

Challenge

Each market opportunity that you consider is not only associated with its own value creation potential but also entails its very own value capture challenge. The challenges are important to understand as they shape how difficult it is to succeed in this market. Note that whereas the Potential was assessed by looking at the market opportunity in and of itself, this dimension examines your own capabilities to succeed in it, and the main obstacles that you may face.

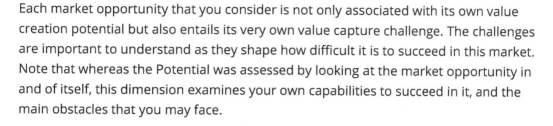

> *In the landscape of market opportunities, where each option is a mountain to be climbed, this dimension refers to your chances of conquering the top of a mountain, rather than its height.*

The Challenge of a market opportunity can be gauged using three main factors:

Implementation obstacles
How difficult will it be for you to create and deliver your offer?

Time to revenue
How long will it take until you can generate cash flow through sales?

External risks
What obstacles in your business environment can stand in your way?

As before, we recommend that you examine each of these factors separately and then combine the scores into an overall Challenge rating.

Implementation obstacles

What does it mean?

On your way to a successful market launch and diffusion of your offering in the market, you will face challenges in creating and delivering the product. Assessing these difficulties will help you in understanding the Challenge associated with a particular market opportunity. Given the resources and capabilities that you already possess, you need to obtain insights on the additional resources and abilities that you will need to develop and acquire in order to succeed with a market opportunity.

How to evaluate?

In order to assess your implementation obstacles, three main questions should be addressed:

How difficult will it be for you to develop the product?
How difficult will it be for you to access the market?
How challenging will it be for you to raise funding for this option?

The answers to these questions offer key insights on the challenges that you will face during implementation. Here are several key questions that can guide you when searching for answers.

Product development difficulties?

☐ Which technological hurdles have to be overcome?

☐ Are there any user-interface and design challenges that you might face?

☐ Are there any regulation requirements that you should comply with?

Sales and distribution difficulties?

☐ What type of distribution channel is required to gain access to customers (direct sales, resellers, retailers etc.)?

☐ Are there adequate channels in place?

☐ How much time will it take to build the channel?

☐ Is it important to have multiple channels?

☐ How costly will it be to operate/ utilise the distribution channel?

☐ Are there effective marketing channels already in place (targeted to your customers)?

☐ How costly will it be to create awareness and interest in your offer (i.e., to acquire new customers)?

Funding challenges?

☐ What amount of money do you need to raise until customers start paying you (i.e., the total seed investment required)?

☐ How difficult will it be for you to raise this amount (availability of money, fashionable sector etc.)?

Important to remember

Innovators often give much thought to the challenges of creating the offering, but neglect the challenges of bringing it to the market. Delivering the offering may sometimes be much more difficult than creating it, so give it careful attention.

Once you understand the challenges in creating and delivering the offering for a particular market opportunity, you can gauge the financial resources required to do so. Adopt a bottom-up analysis when estimating the required funding: How many R&D people will be required? How much do they cost? What type of equipment is required? How many marketing and sales people will you need? How much will that cost? How much money will you need to invest in marketing and sales activities?

If it is not possible to estimate the exact sum of required funding at this stage, try to categorise it as follows: less than 100,000 USD, less than 500,000 USD, less than 2,000,000 USD or more than that. This can provide a sufficient estimation for the financial challenges that lie ahead of you.

Once you have thoroughly gone over these questions, you will be able to score the height of your 'implementation obstacles'. If you find it helpful, you can also score each of the sub-elements separately and then combine their grade into an overall score.

To illustrate the assessment of this factor, let's turn again to Augury's HVAC market for commercial buildings.

Compared to manufacturing equipment, where every machine is unique, the advantage of HVAC equipment lies in its standardisation. Hence, developing a product that can monitor the sounds and vibrations of such a system is much simpler. Augury's founders estimated that it was doable.

Once the product is ready, delivering it to the market will require, at least at the first stage, a direct sales force. This is mainly because the distribution's primary role would be to create demand, rather than to fulfil it.

Over time, however, there will be adequate sales channels that could be used to access this market.

Understanding the development and the sales challenges provided the basis for estimating that the desired seed funding would be around 2 million USD. Overall, the implementation obstacles were therefore classified as 'mid-high'.

 Market Opportunity: *HVAC for Commercial Buildings*

| LOW | MID | HIGH | SUPER HIGH |

IMPLEMENTATION OBSTACLES
Product development difficulties
Sales and distribution difficulties
Funding challenges

Time to revenue

What does it mean?

Positive cash flow is the oxygen of a start-up. The clock is ticking and money is usually burned quickly. The speed with which you can generate cash flow through sales is thus a major consideration. This factor estimates how long it will take until cash begins to accumulate in your account. If the time period is too long, you will likely face key challenges on your innovation path – and will likely experience significant stress, as your key stakeholders, including your employees, may question the viability of your endeavour.

How to evaluate?

To estimate the time to revenue for a market opportunity, you need to consider three main questions:

What is the estimated time for development?
Will we need to wait until the market is ready for our offer?
How long is the sale cycle expected to be?

Based on the answers to these questions, you will have a better understanding of the time element associated with your market opportunity. Several questions can guide you when searching for answers.

Development time?

☐ What are the major milestones that you should accomplish until the product is ready for the market? (think about technological developments, design components, regulation requirements etc.)

☐ How long will it take you to accomplish each milestone?

☐ What is the overall estimated time until the product is ready for the market?

Time between product and market readiness?

☐ After the product is ready, what else should or needs to happen until it can be launched? (Think about value chain elements, required infrastructure, complementary products etc.)

☐ How much time will this take?

☐ Is there a gap in time between product readiness and market readiness? How long is this gap expected to be?

Length of sale cycle?

☐ Who is involved in the buying decision? How many people will you need to talk to/ meet to make a sale?

☐ Are there possible resistances or gate keepers? Why would they resist buying (expensive/ complex/ require change in legacy systems etc.)?

☐ What is the estimated time to make a sale?

☐ What is the estimated deployment time, once a deal is sealed?

Important to remember

A complex and long sale cycle is mostly relevant for B2B markets rather than B2C markets. Consumer markets act differently: while adoption may take time, the actual decision to buy and the deployment of the product are relatively short. However, time considerations are highly critical in both cases.

In addition, time to revenue is closely related to implementation obstacles (assessed above). However, they emphasise two different perspectives that are both important when seeking to understand the underlying Challenge of a market opportunity.

Note that revenues are one key element to measure success in adoption. If your start-up has different success metrics (such as a certain level of traction), you can use them to estimate the required time for adoption.

Once you have thoroughly gone over these questions, you will be able to score the length of 'time to revenue'. If you find it helpful, you can also score each of the sub-elements separately and then combine their grade into an overall score.

Here is how Augury estimated this factor, when evaluating the HVAC market for commercial buildings.

Because the development seemed doable and there were no special regulatory requirements, Gal and Saar estimated that they could launch a product relatively quickly, especially in comparison to the other market opportunities in their set.

The market itself was able to adopt their offering in terms of the required infrastructures, so there was no expected gap between product and market readiness.

The sales cycle, however, is expected to take a while, although deployment can be gradual and there is no need for upfront investment.

Overall, it seems like this market opportunity offers a short time to revenue, scoring well at 'low-mid'.

 Market Opportunity: *HVAC for Commercial Buildings*

LOW		MID	HIGH	SUPER HIGH

TIME TO REVENUE
Development time
Time between product and market readiness
Length of sale cycle

External risks

What does it mean?

The success of your business can be put at risk by many companies and players in your external environment. This risk is often uncontrollable by you, yet it has to be taken into account when assessing how difficult it will be to capture the value inherent in a market opportunity.

How to evaluate?

In order to understand the level of external risks associated with a market opportunity, look at three important questions:

How threatened are you by competition?
How dependent are you on other companies or players?
How susceptive are you to adoption barriers?

An objective answer to these questions will help you to get important insights on the external risks inherent in a market opportunity. Here are some questions that can guide you when searching for answers.

Competitive threat?

☐ Who are your current competitors (name them)?

☐ Who may become your competitor in the future?

☐ How big/ strong are these competitors?

☐ Are there entry barriers for new entrants (patents, regulations, network externalities etc.)?

☐ Do you have a clear advantage over competitors?

☐ Is this advantage sustainable (i.e., unique, difficult to imitate, durable)?

Third party dependencies?

☐ Co-innovation: Who else needs to innovate for your innovation to be successful?

☐ Which other ecosystem players could affect the adoption of your offering? Who else needs to adopt your innovation so that your customers can capture the full value proposition?[o]

☐ Regulation governance: How dependent are you on policy makers and regulators?

Barriers to adoption?

☐ Are the customers receptive to innovations?

☐ Is your product compatible with existing ways of doing things? Existing norms? Existing systems, standards, infrastructure?

☐ How complex is your product?

☐ Can it be tried before purchase?

Important to remember

External risks can be a nerve-wracking element in innovation. In particular, strong competition is often emphasised as a key hazard in the business literature. Yet, while entering a fortified field is dangerous, the lack of competition may be equally worrisome – either the market opportunity you are envisioning is not for real (as others may have discovered and exploited it already) or the lack of competition means that you will carry the burden of educating the market and supplying the complementary elements. So, when assessing external risks associated with the competition, consider the extent to which you have an advantage vis-à-vis the competition. The greater that advantage is, the better your competitive situation. Some even talk about 'unfair' competitive advantage – as such an advantage will help you in making your sale!

As for adoption barriers, remember that some markets adopt innovations more easily than others and that some innovations are more easily adopted.[oo]

To find out more take a look at:
o   The Wide Lens/ Ron Adner (2012)
oo Diffusion of Innovations/ Everett Rogers (1962)

Once you have thoroughly gone over these questions, you will be able to score the level of 'external risks'. If you find it helpful, you can also score each of the sub-elements separately and then combine their grade into an overall score.

Here is how Augury estimated this factor, when evaluating the HVAC market for commercial buildings:

The team's competitive analysis showed that current diagnostic solutions are too costly and too complex. Initial equipment investment can run as high as $50,000, while an even larger investment is required to provide in-house personnel with the required expertise and training for the use of these techniques. Augury's solution is simple to operate and does not require any upfront investment. This gives Augury a clear competitive advantage, which they hope would be a sustainable one – due to patents that they had filed and because they kept on building up their own knowledge and capabilities.

Other than that, their offer is a standalone solution, which means that they are not dependent on any other players in the market or on regulatory governors.

In terms of adoption risks, their product is new and disruptive in a market that is somewhat conservative. However, it will be completely compatible with existing infrastructures, easy to use and available for trials – all factors that lower the barriers for adoption.

Based on these considerations, the level of external risks was rated as 'mid'.

 Market Opportunity: *HVAC for Commercial Buildings*

| LOW | MID | HIGH | SUPER HIGH |

EXTERNAL RISKS
Competitive threat, Third party dependencies,
Barriers to adoption

Challenge: the overall rating

Just as before, once you have thought through all the value capture Challenge factors, you can combine your scores into an overall rating. This rating ranges from 'low' to 'super high', according to the results from your analysis. It will later be used to place the market opportunity on the Attractiveness Map, as Challenge is its X-axis.

Again, an average score can hide information – key downsides or upsides associated with a market opportunity. Yet, it provides one clear measure for comparing alternatives. So, be aware of the individual analysis of each factor and the meaning of a combined score.

Assigning weights to different factors

Are all factors of the same importance? Again, this is a straightforward question with no straightforward answer. We recommend that you carefully observe the different factors and decide how critical they may be to your success.

If you do assign weights, remember that the factors are somewhat interconnected. For example, implementation obstacles and external risks influence time to revenue, although they emphasise different perspectives and important considerations.

In addition, remember to be consistent throughout, and assign the same weights when evaluating other market opportunities.

For Augury, the overall Challenge of pursuing the HVAC opportunity was evaluated as 'mid'. Especially noteworthy was the relatively short time to revenue, which was an important factor for the team. They believed that the implementation obstacles are feasible and the external risks are manageable.

Market Opportunity: *HVAC for Commercial Buildings*

CHALLENGE

LOW	MID	✗ HIGH	SUPER HIGH

IMPLEMENTATION OBSTACLES
Product development difficulties
Sales and distribution difficulties
Funding challenges

LOW ✗	MID	HIGH	SUPER HIGH

TIME TO REVENUE
Development time
Time between product and market readiness
Length of sale cycle

LOW	MI✗	HIGH	SUPER HIGH

EXTERNAL RISKS
Competitive threat
Third party dependencies
Barriers to adoption

OVERALL CHALLENGE

LOW	✗ MID	HIGH	SUPER HIGH

For Microbot Medical, the case is different. Developing the self-cleaning shunts for treating 'water in the brain' condition is quite challenging. Although shunts are synthetic lumens with constant diameter – which makes it easier for a micro-robot to crawl in – the development of such a device bears many obstacles and risks, and takes a long time. Clinical trials are complicated and regulatory demands are challenging. External risks are also quite high, even though competitive offers are inferior. That is due to high dependencies on regulatory governors (such as the FDA) and on insurance reimbursements.

The overall Challenge in pursuing this path was 'high', yet Microbot's management and technology experts were positive about their ability to handle this challenge. Furthermore, the development obstacles, the time to revenue and the external risks were even higher for other market opportunities that the firm considered, as it required the micro-robot to crawl in a biologic lumen with changing diameters (such as blood vessels, the respiratory system, or the digestive tract). Moreover, these high challenges can eventually become major barriers to entry for Microbot's potential competitors in the future.

Key scoring considerations

Scoring your different market opportunities is both a learning and a validation process. It usually begins with assumptions that you hold about the market, and as your knowledge accumulates your understanding relies on an increasing amount of facts. Use Worksheet 2 to generate your key assumptions and to set your key action items as you attempt to find out if an opportunity is real.

Moreover, even if you feel confident with the information that you have gathered about a market opportunity, assigning a score to the different factors and dimensions is often not a trivial task. Here are some important considerations to keep in mind, as you perform this task:

Raising the questions vs. finding the answers

Working with entrepreneurs and innovators, we often hear about their frustrations when seeking to find satisfying answers to market-related questions. It is a complex process, one that does not rely solely on hard data and clear figures, but involves common sense, inductions and some intuition. Yet, the benefit of this process not only lies in finding the right answers but also in asking the right questions.

Hence, the mere fact that you search for answers and that you take these factors into consideration when choosing a market opportunity is important in its own right. In short, try to strive for finding the right answers, but remember that asking the right questions is just as important!

Absolute vs. relative analysis

Should we score a market opportunity in its own right or relative to the other options in our Market Opportunity Set? The answer is 'both'. We recommend that you start assessing an opportunity as a standalone option and score it in absolute terms, but then also think more widely on how it is rated relative to your other options, and adjust the score accordingly, if necessary. Scoring is also a learning process!

Quick and dirty vs. thorough analysis

As stated above, an evaluation process always begins with assumptions that we have about a market opportunity. You can make a 'quick and dirty' evaluation of market opportunities, based on these assumptions. This exercise offers value if you need to shrink your set of opportunities and quickly weed out some options. But even more importantly – you can use this quick evaluation to find out the critical information that you still have to gather, so that you can convert your hypotheses and beliefs into knowledge. Make sure to perform a thorough analysis before you take any action, and base this far-reaching decision on a solid evaluation.

Qualitative vs. quantitative scoring

The natural tendency of entrepreneurs and innovators, especially if they come with an engineering background, is to think about the scoring process in a mathematical way – e.g., transforming the scale into numbers (from 1 to 4) and averaging all numbers to calculate the overall score. While this is a feasible approach, we urge you to think about the assessment in a qualitative manner. Through systematic analysis of the different factors, try to understand the major pros and cons of a market opportunity, and rate its value creation Potential and value capture Challenge accordingly.

Short- vs. long-term horizon

Lastly, the scores that you assign to different factors may depend on the time horizon that you adopt when doing so. A short-term perspective may result in different ratings from those of a long-term perspective, especially due to scaling possibilities over time.

The appropriate time horizon depends largely on your own goals for growing the firm: do you strive to build a large organisation, or do you prefer a quick exit? Whether you adopt a short- or a long-term horizon make sure to be consistent in your approach when assessing all the options in your Market Opportunity Set.

The outcome – your Attractiveness Map

Here we are: once you are done with evaluating each market opportunity in your set, you can place them on the **Attractiveness Map** – and learn about each opportunity and your opportunity set in its totality! The Attractiveness Map allows you to visually depict the evaluation of your market opportunities so you can better grasp their upsides and downsides, and compare them with each other. This visualisation helps you in determining your most attractive options, at a given point in time, so that you can make an informed decision about your Primary Market Opportunity.

The Y-axis of the map represents the 'Potential' of the option, and the X-axis represents its 'Challenge'.

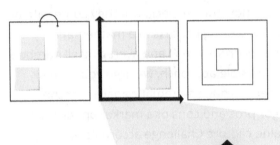

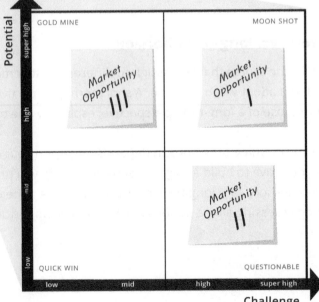

Analysing the Attractiveness Map

The Attractiveness Map unleashes its power once you move your perspective from an individual opportunity to the overall market opportunity set that is placed on it. The map provides you with the ability to compare possible market opportunities, locate the most promising options, and start designing your Agile Focus Strategy.

There are four zones in the Attractiveness Map:

Gold Mine

These are market opportunities with relatively high value creation Potential and low value capture Challenge. In other words: your dream comes true! They are ideally located but relatively rare. A Gold Mine option is usually a result of identifying a significant unmet need – one that no one has addressed before. Or, you may possess unique know-how to overcome a challenging hurdle, one that others simply cannot overcome. If you do have a Gold Mine opportunity, it has the features that would make it your Primary Market Opportunity.

As an example, let's look at Gusto, a US-based start-up founded in 2011, to develop a modern payroll system designed especially for small businesses. The potential of this market opportunity is definitely high. Although there are many payroll solutions, none is tailored specifically to the needs and requirements of small businesses. Gusto's simple and affordable 'one-roof' solution is therefore highly compelling for a large volume market. And even though their pricing is affordable, the economic viability is also high, especially due to customers' stickiness. The overall Challenge is relatively low, although competitive threat should definitely be considered. Implementation obstacles can be dealt with, and the product can be launched in relatively short time. Overall, this high Potential and low-mid Challenge opportunity creates a Gold Mine option. Indeed, in 2015 the company employed over 300 workers, served over 30,000 clients, and was valued for over 1 billion USD.

Moon Shot

These are market opportunities with relatively high value creation Potential but also high value capture Challenge. Truly innovative offers are usually located in this quarter of the Attractiveness Map, bearing high risk and high returns simultaneously. Some investors would argue that these are the most interesting options to invest in, if you believe that the team is qualified to overcome the major challenges that it entails. Hence, Moon Shot options may fit as your Primary Market Opportunity or as a long-term Growth Option.

An interesting example of a Moon Shot opportunity is Given Imaging, a venture that developed a swallowable imaging capsule for endoscopy procedures. Back in 1998 when the firm was founded, the idea of a miniature pill-cam seemed like science fiction, yet the founders believed that a missile technology could be miniaturised to create such a medical product.

While the Potential of this market opportunity was super high (as there was no good solution for examining the small intestine), the Challenge was even higher. Fortunately, the firm succeeded in pursuing this Moon Shot opportunity and launched their first PillCam in 2001. In 2013 Given Imaging held close to 90% market share on gastro-intestinal endoscopy video devices and was acquired for 995 million USD.

Quick Win

These are market opportunities with relatively low value creation Potential and low value capture Challenge. In the risk-return analogy, they represent the low risk/ low return alternatives. They offer limited value creation potential that is relatively safe. These options may offer a great jump-start and may be combined with other opportunities to enhance the long-term potential of the firm. Many innovative firms start by targeting such Quick Win opportunity in the short term – as a stepping stone for a future Moon Shot.

E Ink is a well-known example. Founded in 1997 as a spin-off from the MIT Media Lab, the venture developed a special form of electronic ink that could be used in electronic displays. The founders' vision was to create 'radio paper' – a flexible electronic display that could replace books, magazines and newspapers . . . a clear Moon Shot opportunity. As a short-term option, the firm decided to focus on the large-area signage market.

While this market opportunity suggested a relatively modest potential, it was also much less challenging, especially in terms of the technological obstacles that still needed to be solved (as the initial ink only worked in blue and white). Overall, E Ink perceived this opportunity to be its best stepping stone. Reality, however, proved to be different: manufacturing costs were significantly above expectations, the firm had to invest a lot in building a sales force as the distribution channel, and the customers themselves did not like the blue and white limitation.[o]

Tesla's Roadster – its initial luxury, all electric sports car – is another example. While clearly challenging, it is still easier to build a luxurious $100,000 car that draws on the latest technological advances in electric vehicle technology than a model geared towards the mass market that would have needed to be much cheaper. Tesla aimed to target this niche market, although it had a lower potential, as a stepping stone for technologically more advanced and more affordable models that were Moon Shots at that time.

Questionable

These are market opportunities with relatively low value creation Potential and high value capture Challenge. It is no surprise that this is the least desirable quadrant. While you will likely be better off finding a target market opportunity in a different quarter, you might just want to keep these Questionable opportunities in mind, as conditions may change over time and they may turn into more attractive opportunities at some point in the future.

Many venture projects fail because they pursue a Questionable opportunity, often without even being aware of that! As studies show, they run into the problem of having little or no demand for the product that they have built with much sweat: there is not a sufficiently compelling value proposition or the market size is simply too limited. This is exactly what low Potential and high Challenge opportunity means. In fact, in a post mortem analysis of 101 start-up failures done by CB Insights, the number one reason for failure (in 42% of all cases) was that the start-ups primarily addressed problems that are interesting to solve rather than problems that serve a market need.[oo]

Once you map your opportunities, you can use these distinctive quarters to easily discriminate your options and grasp their differences.

To find out more take a look at:

o   E Ink in 2005/ Yoffie & Mack, HBS case (2005)

oo The Top 20 Reasons Startups Fail/ CB Insights (2014)

Let's examine the Attractiveness Map of Augury.

The evaluation of the HVAC opportunity for commercial buildings resulted in an overall rating of high Potential and mid Challenge. Hence, looking at the Attractiveness Map, it is located in the desirable Gold Mine quarter.
Augury had four other market opportunities that they wanted to evaluate, before making such an important decision.

The first one was predictive maintenance for manufacturing lines in different factories. Manufacturers can benefit greatly from preventing catastrophic failures, thus decreasing downtime and saving energy and operational costs.

However, it turns out that every line is unique and requires a great deal of customisation. Overall, this was an opportunity with high Potential and high Challenge.

The second market opportunity was international freight companies with cooling containers.

Analysis showed that this market had a mid-level of Potential, especially since the value of predictive maintenance was not big enough.

The Challenge, however, was manageable and was rated as 'mid-high'.

Cooling containers

WORKSHEET 2
EVALUATE MARKET OPPORTUNITY ATTRACTIVENESS   NAME *Augury*

Use this worksheet for every market opportunity you would like to evaluate.

Market Opportunity: *Cooling containers*

POTENTIAL

COMPELLING REASON TO BUY — MID
Unmet need
Effective solution
Better than current solutions

MARKET VOLUME — MID/HIGH
Current market size
Expected growth

ECONOMIC VIABILITY — MID/HIGH
Margins (value vs. cost)
Customers' ability to pay
Customer stickiness

OVERALL POTENTIAL — MID

CHALLENGE

IMPLEMENTATION OBSTACLES — MID/HIGH
Product development difficulties
Sales and distribution difficulties
Funding challenges

TIME TO REVENUE — MID
Development time
Time between product and market readiness
Length of sale cycle

EXTERNAL RISKS — MID/HIGH
Competitive threat
Third party dependences
Barriers to adoption

OVERALL CHALLENGE — MID/HIGH

Use the overall ratings to situate each market opportunity on the Attractiveness Map.

95

The third option was white appliances. Augury believed that once the internet is embedded in these appliances, they could offer manufacturers to install their device in these appliances.

Although the compelling reason to buy is not extremely high (because the cost of a breakdown is relatively low), the market volume is huge and economically worthwhile, so the overall Potential is rated as 'high'.

However, the market was just not ready yet for that type of offering, so time to revenue and external risks were 'super high', resulting in a high Challenge level.

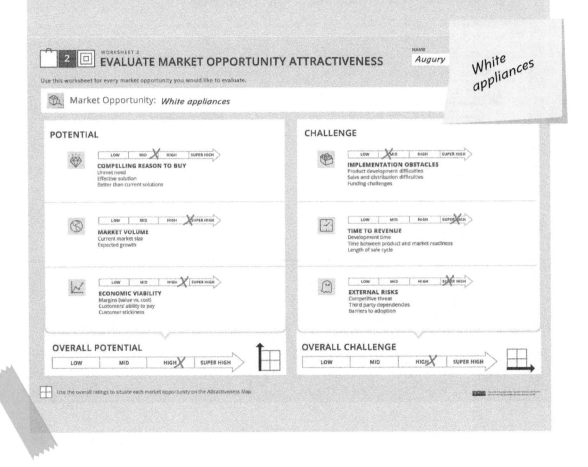

Lastly, Augury's founders wanted to check the opportunity to offer predictive maintenance capabilities for cars – by offering 'Augury inside' to car manufacturers.

This market opportunity had a 'super-high' Potential, but also entailed 'super-high' Challenge, especially due to implementation obstacles and extremely long time to revenue.

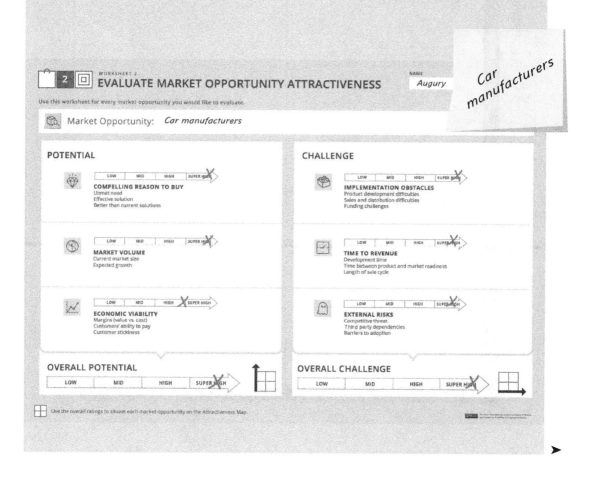

The learning and evaluation process that Augury's team engaged in can now be summarised visually with the Attractiveness Map. This map enables them to capture the upsides and downsides of each individual opportunity, and relative to others.

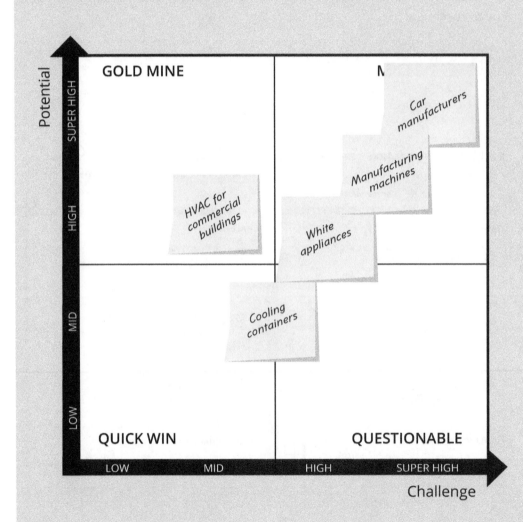

What can we learn from the Attractiveness Map?

The Attractiveness Map is designed to help you in making your optimal choice of market opportunities. As highlighted, it helps you to understand each opportunity in and of itself – and in relation to other opportunities. It can thus offer vital insights on the growth possibilities that lie ahead!

Analysing each individual market opportunity

As you look at the position of each market opportunity individually, you can better grasp its downsides and upsides, and understand the trade-offs that it bears.

Analysing the set of market opportunities

Looking at the bigger picture, the map will show you how superior or inferior an opportunity is relative to others and how your opportunities are spread across the different quarters. While highly attractive market opportunities represent great target market opportunities, variety across quadrants is desirable – as it allows you to balance the downsides of your Primary Market Opportunity by keeping other options open.

Choosing a preferred market opportunity (the Primary Market Opportunity)

By zooming in on each individual market opportunity, and then zooming out on the whole set of opportunities, you will obtain important insights that will allow you to choose your preferred market opportunity, the one that you plan to pursue with full force: your Primary Market Opportunity. This choice is actually the first step in building your Agile Focus Strategy, as will be described in the next chapter.

Shaping a market opportunity to improve its location on the Attractiveness Map

The characteristics of a market opportunity are not written in stone. You can change them so that the opportunity becomes more attractive and/ or is fraught with fewer challenges. Ultimately, by shaping the opportunity, you can attain a better position on the Attractiveness Map. So don't wait until someone else 'moves your cheese' – try to do it yourself!

Shaping a market opportunity to improve its location on the map requires a fresh look at its major downsides and risks, and at any untapped potential. Here are a few proven ways that will help you in shaping your market opportunity – and, ultimately, creating more 'Gold Mines' in your set of market opportunities.

Improving the 'Potential' of a market opportunity:

Often, an unsatisfying score here relates to a low level of (expected) market demand. It could be because the 'pain' you are addressing is not significantly strong, or simply because not many customers face this pain. One way to deal with this situation is to try to think differently about your market and re-segment it in another way, so that you aim for a (sub-)segment that feels a stronger pain and/ or is significantly larger. For example, if you offer an environmental monitoring solution for hospitals, you can segment this market based on private vs. public hospitals, but you can also sub-segment it according to the size of specific departments within the hospital.

Improving the 'Challenge' of a market opportunity:

Many obstacles can stand in your way when you attempt to capture value from a market opportunity. It could be major difficulties in developing or delivering your offer, or major risks within your business environment. Try to think if there is anything you can do to diminish this risk or handle these obstacles over time, so that the value capture Challenge decreases. One way to accomplish this is to find a strategic partner or an ally that could help you overcome your weaknesses. For example, cooperating with another player in the value chain may help you in overcoming the challenges in developing a product, reduce your external dependencies on others or shorten your time to revenue.

? FAQs

Are these the only parameters that one should consider when evaluating a market opportunity? Are there others?

You can definitely think of other parameters that are not listed in Worksheet 2 and that may influence the attractiveness of a market opportunity. Nevertheless, Worksheet 2 contains a comprehensive list of factors that cover the key considerations for most cases. If you do think, however, that there are other factors that require your attention, feel free to add and weigh them as you determine the overall Potential or Challenge scores for a market opportunity. Notably, there are some additional factors that do not influence these two dimensions, but may influence your choice, such as your own values, aspirations and passion. We will further elaborate on these factors in the next chapter, where we discuss how to choose your Primary Market Opportunity.

My goal is quick exit so some of my parameters are different – what should I do?

Naturally, you should evaluate your opportunities according to the goals that you want to accomplish. Our set of evaluation parameters was designed with the primary goal in mind to build a successful and growing venture or to successfully commercialise an innovation over time. If you build your venture with a primary goal of exiting quickly, your evaluation parameters may change. So, feel free to add or revise some factors according to your goal, when evaluating the Potential and the Challenge of an opportunity. In case you do that, make sure to be consistent and rate all your opportunities based on the same parameters.

Prior experience of the founders in a specific market is a very important parameter. Why is it missing in the evaluation?

Prior experience in a specific market domain can be a great advantage. You already possess customer intimacy that enables you to better understand their needs and how to reach them, and you also probably have a good network for building the necessary ecosystem in the market. The influence of such prior experience is therefore reflected in a lower Challenge for capturing value. Thus, prior experience is not an evaluation parameter in and of itself, but will influence how you score other important factors.

Is it possible to evaluate and compare different market domains rather than different market opportunities?

As mentioned before, we call this concern the 'continents vs. countries' analysis. A continent, for this matter, is a broad market domain, such as medical device or surveillance, for example. A country within a continent is a more specific market segment within this domain, such as cardiologists or radiologists in the medical field. Sometimes, an initial decision requires the evaluation of broad domains, or continents, first. While it is possible to use Worksheet 2 to assess the attractiveness of a market domain, it is worthwhile doing so only if the segments within this domain are somewhat similar. If there is high variation across different market segments, the average scoring of a broad market domain will likely lead to biased conclusions.

Our opportunity involves a two-sided platform. How can we evaluate it?

In a two-sided platform model, such as AirBnB, the firm creates value primarily by enabling direct interactions between two distinct groups of users. Such 'marketplace' platforms incur costs in serving both groups and can collect revenues from each (although sometimes one side is subsidised). To succeed in a multi-sided platform, you actually need to make sure that you provide value to each side and that you can overcome the challenges of serving each side. Therefore, we recommend that you perform a separate evaluation for each type of user, based on Worksheet 2, and then combine these evaluations to an overall score of the market opportunity. The most logical way to combine ratings in this case is to take the lowest score of both sides in each of the two dimensions: Potential and Challenge.

Can social ventures benefit from Worksheet 2 as well?

The assessment done in Worksheet 2 examines the economic potential of an option. Social ventures, however, strive to achieve financial returns as well as social impact. The Potential of such market opportunities, therefore, should be examined from both ends: the expected economic gains as well as the expected social gains. Hence, if you are assessing such an option, we recommend that you add to the Potential dimension another factor: the extent to which this opportunity solves a social problem and, thus, provides social benefits. Likewise, the Challenge dimension may entail factors that are unique to capturing social benefits. In the end, make sure to be consistent and rate all your opportunities based on the same parameters.

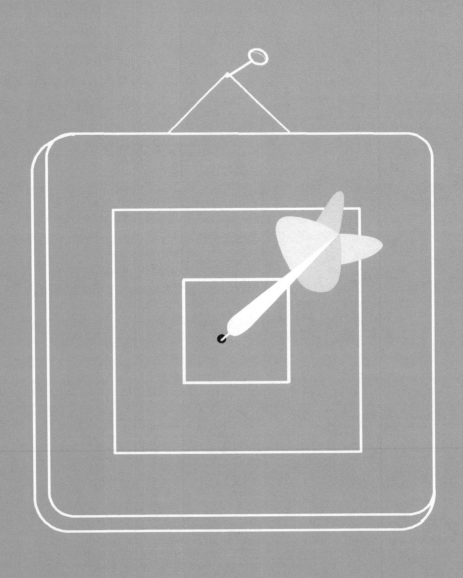

2.3 Agile Focus Dartboard

The discovery of new market opportunities and their assessment is an important learning process for you. Hence, take your time – it may take several weeks, or even more. Yet at some point it is time to make a decision:

What market opportunities should you focus on?

Without a doubt, this is one of the most fundamental decisions you will ever make in your commercialisation process: not only is it key for getting traction on the marketplace and for creating value, but it also shapes the DNA of the company that you are establishing.

Yet, here is the catch: despite the critical nature of this choice and your best efforts in finding the most fertile ground for your innovation, you may still have to adapt your choice over time! This is what innovation is all about: due to the uncertainty inherent in your decision, you better just accept that change is a likely outcome – and get ready for it! In other words: prepare for the time when unforeseen things happen . . .

What does this all mean in practical terms?

A smart market opportunity strategy has to take into account two major aspects:

1 **What** *are the most attractive market opportunities that you should focus on?*

2 **How** *can you focus, yet stay flexible, agile and open-minded at the same time?*

The **Agile Focus Strategy** is your way to combine these two aspects to set an optimal strategy and reap the greatest value from your commercialisation efforts.

Agile Focus Strategy: Combining focus & flexibility

The Agile Focus Strategy balances the tension between focus and flexibility, by consciously keeping open other market opportunities: those that will allow you to mitigate your risk and to increase your value with minimum effort.

Hence, this strategy enables you to leverage your resources and capabilities, so that you allocate them more effectively and avoid a potentially fatal lock-in. Don't get trapped!

The Agile Focus Strategy has significant implications for how you build and design your venture. It will enable you to focus on the most attractive market opportunity on one hand, while maintaining your agility and manoeuvrability on the other.

How can this be achieved?

There is a lot you can do to keep some options open now and to nurture your agility, without losing the focus that is required to push forward on your most attractive path! In particular, you can develop your resources and capabilities in a way that allows for greater flexibility down the road – for instance, by creating modularised technology that can be reconfigured more easily, by casting a wider Intellectual Property (IP) net, or by picking a brand name that would lend itself for redirection. These relatively low investments will make your firm more robust to change, without compromising the pursuit of your most promising opportunity.

> *In the landscape of market opportunities where each mountain represents a possible option, your Agile Focus Strategy can create 'bridges' between the mountain you are currently climbing, and the ones around it, so that you will avoid starting a new climb from the very bottom if change is required.*

In entrepreneurship, keeping options open is akin to the Real Options reasoning: a relatively small investment now provides you with the right – but not the obligation – to further pursue the opportunity in the future.

The Agile Focus Strategy, therefore, builds on the logic of **Real Options** that was developed in research on strategising under uncertainty.

🔍 Research insights

The theory of real options concerns classes of investments in real assets that are similar to financial options in structure. Just as the purchase of a financial option contract conveys the right, but not the obligation, to purchase its underlying asset in the future, investment in a real option conveys the opportunity to continue investment in the future should conditions prove favourable. If further investment is not desired, the cost of failure is limited to the cost of creating the real option.°

But what about 'laser-sharp' focusing?

Entrepreneurs are often told that they have to pursue a narrowly focused strategy, or else they won't be able to survive. And the reason for this advice is fairly clear: small ventures are scarce on resources (think about the limited human and financial capital) and, thus, they must not spread their efforts too thinly.

While this is all very true, it neglects the importance of agility, which is especially critical for operating under conditions of uncertainty. In fact, our comprehensive research of over 500 start-ups clearly showed the inherent trade-offs in laser-sharp focusing.

° To find out more take a look at: Strategy through the option lens: An integrated view of resource investments and the incremental-choice process/ Bowman & Hurry (1993); A real options logic for initiating technology positioning investments/ Rita McGrath (1997); Investment Under Uncertainty/ Dixit & Pindyck (1994)

Q Research insights

How should entrepreneurs manage the delicate balance between staying focused and staying flexible? Intrigued by this question, we have studied more than 500 technology ventures over the past 10 years.**o**
Here are some of our findings:

☐ Most firms change their initial market choice over time, so learning how to balance between focus and flexibility is absolutely crucial.

☐ A laser-sharp focus on one market opportunity doesn't pay off for most firms! Consciously keeping related market options open is key for enhancing flexibility and driving success.

☐ Market opportunities that are closely related (and thus do not require significant additional investments nor a lot of additional bandwidth by the entrepreneurs) may even be pursued in parallel – increasing the chances of success amid high market uncertainty.

Stephen Kaufer, co-founder of TripAdvisor, emphasises the downside of laser-sharp focusing in some advice he offers to entrepreneurs:

. . . if you are lightning focused on just one thing and aren't willing to consider others, you probably don't have the flexibility to make it when things don't go according to plan. That's the one truism: things won't go according to plan∞

To find out more take a look at:
o Market entry decisions, emergence processes & adaptation in new organizations/ Tal, Gruber & de Haan (Dissertation Technion)
oo Founders at Work/ Jessica Livingston (2008)

How to design your Agile Focus Strategy?

The assessment accomplished in Worksheet 2 and the Attractiveness Map is the basis for designing your Agile Focus Strategy. It shows you how attractive your options are – both each by itself and in relation to others. This important information will help you choose your Primary Market Opportunity – the one that you will be pursuing with full force.

However, setting a smart strategy is not only based on finding the most attractive opportunity but also on creating a smart portfolio around it to enhance flexibility. To do so, you will need to pick from your Market Opportunity Set at least one Backup Option and one Growth Option.

 A Backup Option is an attractive market opportunity that does not share the same major risks of your Primary Market Opportunity. It allows you to change direction over time, if necessary.

 A Growth Option is an attractive market opportunity that allows you to create additional value over time.

Backup and Growth Options should ideally be closely related to your Primary Market Opportunity: product and market relatedness will allow you to leverage your existing resources, capabilities and relationships – thereby increasing your value creation and balancing your risk with *minimum effort*. You can keep your Backup and Growth Options open (for pursuing them later if you desire to do so), or you can even decide to pursue them now, parallel to your Primary Market Opportunity. This investment decision depends on the additional effort that is required for pursuing the options, and on how critical they are for your venture's survival or success.

The result of this design process is your Agile Focus Strategy: it clearly states your Primary Market Opportunity/ ies, the options that you keep open as Backup or Growth and the opportunities that you currently keep in 'storage' and disregard at this stage.

You can depict your strategy and communicate it with the Agile Focus Dartboard.

Reid Hoffman is the co-founder and executive chairman of LinkedIn and a partner at Greylock Partners Venture Capital. In his essay on Pitch Advice for Entrepreneurs, he emphasises the importance of having Backup Options at hand:

> *. . . you want to show focus in your decks by emphasizing what you're really betting on. However, show some maneuverability.*
> *Don't just say that you have five different options. Instead, say that you're doing one, but you also have some fall-back or maneuvering options.*
>
> *For example, if we were doing the Series B pitch in 2004 with my knowledge of today, we would emphasize that LinkedIn would start by transforming one business – the recruiting industry, by shifting it from a posting model to a searching model. Then, in our talking points, we would highlight some of the other businesses we can transform with our platform.*
>
> *Invest in A, but here's B to show that we could contain that risk. Investors would appreciate this because you're identifying a reasonable risk and demonstrating that you have actually thought about what you would do if the primary plan doesn't play out as you expect.*°

A clear roadmap for your market opportunities will not only help you in balancing your risk but will also help you in dealing with opportunistic options that tend to pop up along the way, as you can more easily evaluate and categorise them based on the firm's Agile Focus Strategy.

° To find out more take a look at: www.reidhoffman.org/485-business-and-entrepeneurship/2135-linkedin-s-series-b-pitch-to-greylock

Your main takeaways

Designing your Agile Focus Strategy is the last step of the Market Opportunity Navigator, and it is actually the main outcome of this whole process. It enables you to focus on the most attractive market opportunity and at the same time to build your agility in preparation for a world full of uncertainty. Note, however, that your Agile Focus is not merely a strategy, it is also a *mindset*. We urge you to adopt this mindset from the very early stages of your innovation effort:

First and foremost, this mindset entails cognitive flexibility. It's not only about the flexibility of your resources and capabilities, and their ability to serve different market needs. It is also about your own openness and receptiveness to alternative opportunities and to change or adaptation. This is very important, as cognitive rigidity may lead you very quickly into the graveyard of companies that failed to listen to the market and to adapt promptly. Designing a smart portfolio by keeping your Backup and Growth Options open actually helps you to build and maintain the cognitive flexibility of you and your team, regardless of whether you will actually pursue these options when the time comes.

An Agile Focus mindset also means that you don't rush your focus decision. Although many talk about the importance of focusing from day one, Agile Focusing actually implies that you take your time to investigate and to get acquainted with different market opportunities, and can make your decision carefully! Don't rush to scale up too quickly, as it just may be that you are striving to conquer the wrong market.

Yet, at some point you will need to set your focusing strategy. This is not an easy task. The most difficult part is to figure out what not to do. Letting go of potentially interesting opportunities is often the most painful part of this process. Yet, if you adopt the Agile Focus mindset, it becomes less challenging.

You can understand by now that the 'perfect' market opportunity is probably not yet revealed. In fact, it is very likely that you have not found the 'perfect' market opportunity to focus on, simply because there rarely is a 'perfect' one. However, by now you have taken into account all the major considerations and utilised all the information that you have in hand, to set the optimal strategy for the time being. And if, for any reason, it turns out to be the wrong decision, you are prepared for change and adaptation.

WORKSHEET 3:
DESIGN YOUR AGILE FOCUS STRATEGY

Build a smart portfolio around your Primary Market Opportunity to mitigate your risk and increase your value.

I Choose a Primary Market Opportunity to focus on (based on the Attractiveness Map).

II Pick other attractive market opportunities from your set to examine possible Backup and Growth Options.

Relatedness to your Primary Market Opportunity:

PRODUCT RELATEDNESS
To what extent do the products share: technological competences, required resources, necessary networks

MARKET RELATEDNESS
To what extent do the customers share: values and benefits, sales channels, word-of-mouth

Suitable as:

BACKUP OPTION
Attractive market opportunities that do not share major risks with your Primary Market Opportunity to allow for a change in direction

☐ Backup

GROWTH OPTION
Attractive market opportunities that allow your business to create additional value

☐ Growth

III Design your Agile Focus Strategy:
☐ Keep at least one Backup and one Growth Option open
☐ Decide if any option is worth pursuing now
☐ Place the rest in storage

| Pursue now | Keep open | Place in storage |

Mark your strategy on the Agile Focus Dartboard.

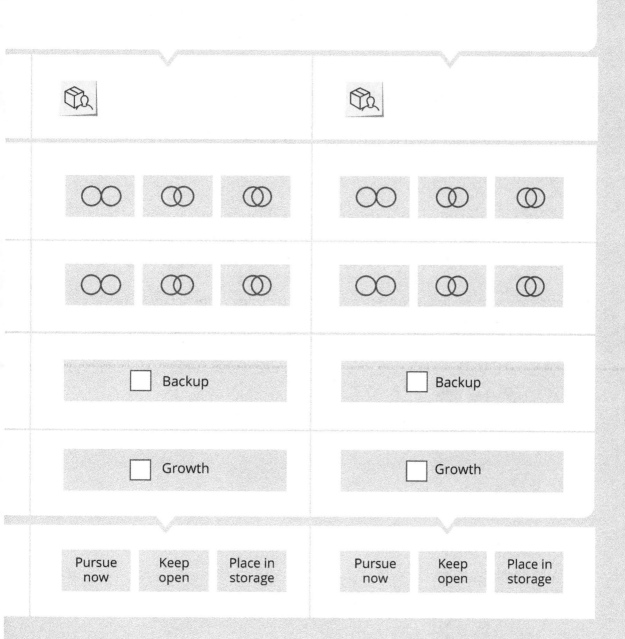

Backup

Growth

Backup

Growth

| Pursue now | Keep open | Place in storage | | Pursue now | Keep open | Place in storage |

WORKSHEET 3:
Designing your Agile Focus Strategy

Worksheet 3 helps you to design your Agile Focus Strategy. Specifically, once you choose your Primary Market Opportunity, it will assist you in finding the best Backup Options and Growth Options, based on their attractiveness and their relatedness to your primary opportunity.

You will then need to decide how much effort you are currently going to invest in these options: will you pursue them now, in parallel to your primary opportunity, or will you just keep them open (i.e., in order to pursue them in the future)? The result of this process is your Agile Focus Strategy, which can then be depicted on the Agile Focus Dartboard.

> *If you are unsure what your Primary Market Opportunity should be, use a separate worksheet for each possible candidate. This scenario-playing will help you to eventually determine your strategy!*

The design of your Agile Focus Strategy begins with choosing your Primary Market Opportunity. Once this is set, you can start planning your smart portfolio of Backup and Growth Options.

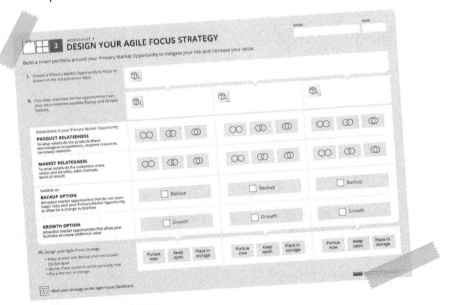

Step 1: Choosing your Primary Market Opportunity

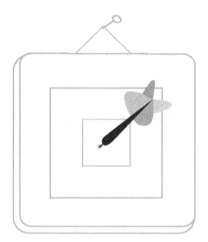

The Primary Market Opportunity is the option that you want to focus on.
The one that you will pursue with full force, investing most of your resources and capabilities in conquering it.

Having several exciting opportunities at hand may feel like visiting a candy store. The candies all look tasty and colourful, but if you try to eat them all you will end up feeling awful. Your challenge is, therefore, to control yourself and decide which candy is the best one for you. You cannot pursue too many opportunities in parallel, or you may end up really sick . . .

Choosing your Primary Market Opportunity is sometimes a clear and straightforward decision, but it could also be a difficult and even frustrating decision, as you are forced to let go of other seemingly interesting alternatives, and you are really not sure which one should eventually win your attention.

To make a smart choice, you first need to examine the Attractiveness Map and utilise all the knowledge that you have gathered from the evaluation process. Note that there may be unique considerations in your case that may not be reflected in the Attractiveness Map, such as your personal inclinations, or the inclinations of your stakeholders.

Attractiveness Map considerations

The independent evaluation of each market opportunity and the overall picture that the Attractiveness Map offers provide you with a deep understanding of which opportunities are superior to others. Based on their Potential level and on their Challenge level you can compare alternative options and choose your Primary Market Opportunity.

Sometimes the map provides a clear answer that simplifies this choice. This happens when a single option is more attractive than all the others. But in other cases, the location of your options on the Attractiveness Map does not provide a straightforward answer.

Here are some common patterns of the Attractiveness Map, and how they may influence the choice of your Primary Market Opportunity:

1. One clearly superior opportunity

If you have a single opportunity located in the Gold Mine quarter, your choice is relatively easy. Other less attractive opportunities may still be important, as they may serve as your Growth or Backup Options.

2. Diagonal trade-off

Diagonal trade-off is a very common pattern, in which your options are spread along the 'risk-return' diagonal: some are low risk-low return opportunities, located in the Quick Win quarter, and some are high risk-high return options, located in the Moon Shot quarter. A preferred market opportunity in this case is not readily apparent. You can choose to begin with a smaller option, which would serve as a stepping stone for a larger one in the future, or you can shoot for the moon from the very beginning. This choice depends, among others, on your personal preferences, your propensity for risk, the interest of your stakeholders, and on the resources that you have in hand or may likely acquire.

3. Options are all closely located

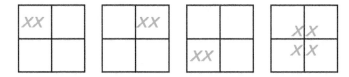

In some cases, options are not spread across the map, but are all situated in the same quarter: the Gold Mine, the Quick Win, or the Moon Shot. Alternatively, they can all be scattered around the middle. In these cases, the best option is not apparent, as opportunities are not too distinctive in their Potential and their Challenge.

Choosing your Primary Market Opportunity in this situation may heavily depend on your personal preferences and the interest of your stakeholders, or on specific factors in Worksheet 2 that seem most important to you (such as time to revenue for example). Additionally, some options may still be better positioned than others – even if they are closely positioned. So choose the option that is relatively more promising, or the one which you believe can be shaped to become more attractive in the future.

4. No attractive options

Unfortunately, this may happen as well. After a thorough assessment you may find yourself with opportunities that are not sufficiently attractive. If all your options are located in the Questionable quarter, you could do one of two things: either go back to Worksheet 1, and try to identify additional market opportunities, or think how to shape one of your options to improve its location on the Attractiveness Map.

Although sometimes inevitable, we do recommend that your Primary Market Opportunity should not be positioned in the Questionable zone. Think twice, even three times if you want to take this difficult road that is likely to lead to outcomes that might not warrant your efforts!

Other considerations

The Attractiveness Map depicts the objective evaluation of your market opportunities, based on their Potential and Challenge. However, there are other important considerations that may come into play when choosing your Primary Market Opportunity.

Personal fit with the opportunity

You (and your founding team) have to see if the opportunity matches your personal preferences: your values, your passion, your aspirations, and even your attitude towards risk taking. Our colleague John Mullins describes the team's mission, aspiration and propensity to risk as very important parameters for evaluating a business opportunity.°
You should therefore choose your primary market not only because it has the highest Potential or the lowest Challenge but also because you love it, and will continue to love it as your venture grows and evolves. Some term this important aspect 'product/ market/ founder fit': success is not only driven by building something that people actually want, it is also derived from doing something that YOU actually enjoy doing!

Fit with stakeholders' interest

Sometimes you already have key stakeholders that have to be considered when choosing your Primary Market Opportunity. These may be current investors, existing partners etc. Their incentives and interest may not be completely aligned with yours, but they still have to be considered. For example, if your existing investors come from a specific market domain, they may push you to choose an opportunity within this domain. If you do not like their preferences, the Navigator gives you substantiated insights that may help you in redirecting their interest to another market domain.
In other cases, investors may heavily weigh your 'time to revenue', as they need to realise their investment in a relatively short time frame, and therefore tilt your choice in a specific direction.

Resource constraints

Sometimes you just have to start with a Quick Win option, simply because you don't have the resources to pursue a larger, more challenging opportunity. Add your current financial and human capital to the equation when choosing your Primary Market Opportunity.

° To find out more take a look at: The New Business Road Test/ John Mullins (2006)

When is the right time to make this decision?

Don't rush making this profound decision. Take your time to discover manifold market opportunities and to research them as thoroughly as possible, as you may end up running with full force in the wrong direction. In fact, a recent study by Startup Genome found that 74% of internet start-ups fail due to premature scaling, that is, expending money and resources without consistent evidence for potential growth. Moreover, they found that start-ups need two to three times longer to validate their market than most founders expect. This underestimation creates the pressure to scale prematurely.°

So take the time to develop your strategy. At some point, however, it is necessary to decide what market opportunity you are going to focus on. How do you know that this time has arrived?

When learning reaches a point of saturation

At some point you may feel that any additional information is familiar to you. There is nothing new . . . This means that you have reached saturation. Staying in the learning phase is thus no longer productive. This does not mean that you have kicked uncertainty out of your field. Some questions may still be open, but simply be un-answerable at this point. It's time to take the decision, as difficult as it may be.

When you are running out of money (oxygen!)

For start-ups, money means oxygen. When you have to raise money, you will need to decide on your Primary Market Opportunity. Most investors want to see a clear strategy, and will most likely decide on whether to invest in your venture based on the opportunity that you intend to pursue initially, as well as other opportunities that you can exploit over time.

When you have to invest in branding

The firm's branding often implies its markets and applications (think about 'GetTaxi', as one clear example). Investing in brand development requires quite a lot of resources, and changing your brand name requires even more . . . So once you need to start branding, you better have a clear understanding about your Primary Market Opportunity as well as your Agile Focus Strategy. Alternatively, you may adapt a broader brand name (such as Amazon for example), that would still give you the flexibility to manoeuvre over time.

A few tips for making this profound decision

There is no 'perfect' option

Market opportunities differ in terms of their features and it is most likely that you don't find the 'perfect' market opportunity. They all tend to have upsides and downsides. For some, the upsides outweigh the downsides, yet there rarely is a 'perfect' option. Once you accept this, and understand the drawbacks that you are about to confront, it is easier to make a decision.

Make it a team decision

One of the biggest values of the Market Opportunity Navigator is that it gives you and your team the possibility to clearly discuss the all-important market opportunity choice with a crisp language. The Market Opportunity Navigator is your communication tool! A team discussion brings different perspectives to the table and takes into account the personal inclinations of others. Furthermore, a decision that was made together will increase the team's motivation to invest all their efforts, and, much more than that, to succeed at it.

Back to Augury:

As we have seen, Augury's Attractiveness Map included five options. It was now time to decide which one will be their primary market. This was not an easy decision: they all had some major upsides and downsides.

Examining the Attractiveness Map revealed that cooling containers are just not interesting enough for the firm and that cars would be too far out to begin with. It seemed that HVAC for commercial buildings – which was the only option located in the Gold Mine quarter – was indeed the most attractive option, especially when emphasising the time to revenue factor – which was very important to the team.

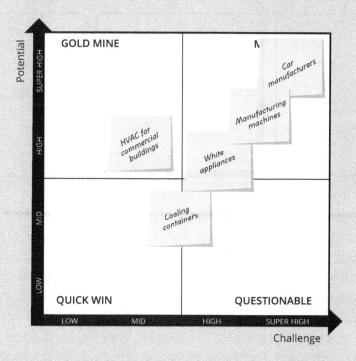

The founders decided to initially focus on offering predictive maintenance solutions to large commercial buildings operating heating, ventilation and air-conditioning systems.

Let's examine another example, where the options were all closely scattered around the middle. KalOptics was a US-based start-up. Its technology provided a simple to use, cost-effective method of capturing, manipulating and editing photorealistic textured materials, thus making 3D computer-generated imagery indistinguishable from the original.

The markets for KalOptics' products included visual effects in movies, animation and gaming, catalogues and advertisers, as well as designers (for improved renderings by interior, fashion, architectural and industrial designers). A thorough analysis of these four different market opportunities revealed little distinction between their Potential level and their Challenge level. In other words, while each option had its own pros and cons, they were all located close to each other in the middle part of the Attractiveness Map.

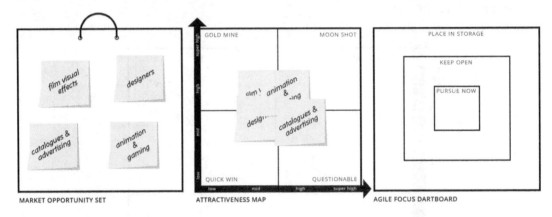

MARKET OPPORTUNITY SET   ATTRACTIVENESS MAP   AGILE FOCUS DARTBOARD

In this case, the visual map itself cannot provide the required prioritisation for choosing the most attractive opportunity. It is necessary to go back to the details of Worksheet 2 to better distinguish the options. In the case of KalOptics, one thing became clear as they assessed their opportunities and talked with potential customers: the market for visual effects in movies, while definitely not the largest, was the most appropriate one to begin with, as movie makers were already spending enormous amounts on visual effects and were ready to adopt the firm's solution. They were also considered to be 'lead users' in rendering textured surfaces, so that other industries looked up to them in a search for solutions. Hence, the firm decided to focus on film studios as their initial target market.

Once you have chosen your Primary Market Opportunity, mark it on the upper part of Worksheet 3. It is now possible to plan your portfolio of Backup and Growth Options.

Step 2:
Examining possible Backup and Growth Options

The main objective of the Agile Focus Strategy is to balance your risk and to increase your value creation with minimum effort.

To do that, you will need to pick at least one market opportunity as your possible Backup Option and one market opportunity as your possible Growth Option, to create a smart portfolio around your Primary Market Opportunity!

A **Backup Option** allows you to change direction over time. It answers the question: **If we are not successful, what shall we do next?**

A **Growth Option** allows you to create additional value over time. It answers the question: **If we are successful, what shall we do next?**

To identify possible candidates for your Agile Focus portfolio, go back to the Attractiveness Map and the evaluations you have done in Worksheet 2. Pick other attractive market opportunities – those that you would like to consider in more detail as your candidates – and list them in the designated spot in Worksheet 3.

Sometimes, you can also consider additional market opportunities that had originally not been placed in your set of options, but that now – after you have chosen your Primary Market Opportunity – appear to be interesting options as they are related to your main market. If this is the case, you can analyse these options as candidates for your Agile Focus portfolio, but don't forget to add them to your Market Opportunity Set as well, as they will require additional evaluation.

Next, you will check how related these options are to your Primary Market Opportunity, and whether they are suitable to become your Backup or Growth Options. The more related they are, the less the effort required to keep them open.

Assessing the relatedness to your Primary Market Opportunity

Relatedness of two market opportunities means that you can effectively leverage the resources, capabilities and relationships that you are developing for one option for succeeding in the other.

When building a smart portfolio around your Primary Market Opportunity, it is important that your Backup Option and Growth Option will be as related as possible to your primary market. In this case, the additional effort that will be required to pursue them will be relatively low.

To assess the ability to leverage your resources and capabilities from one option to another, two types of relatedness need to be examined: Product Relatedness and Market Relatedness.

Product Relatedness
is the extent to which the development of the two products requires similar resources and capabilities.

Market Relatedness
is the extent to which the marketing and distribution of the two products require similar resources and capabilities.

Both types of relatedness are equally important considerations. However, while entrepreneurs tend to consider product relatedness, they often neglect examining market relatedness. This may turn out to be a critical mistake, as developing the competences to play in a 'distant' or unrelated market may require huge efforts that a small venture simply cannot afford.

Assessing product relatedness

The development of your product (or your offering in a more general sense) requires specific capabilities, resources and networks.

To examine the level of relatedness between the product associated with your Primary Market Opportunity and the product associated with your potential Backup/ Growth Option, think about the following questions:

To what extent do the products share . . .

 Technological competences?
(i.e., products' functions and features rely on similar technological developments and share regulation requirements)

 Required resources?
(i.e., employees, manufacturing equipment, intellectual property etc.)

 Necessary networks?
(i.e., suppliers, partners or other members of the value chain)

The overall product relatedness can then be rated as one of three levels:

  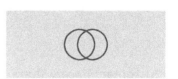

Products hardly share
not related

Products share little
somewhat related

Products share a lot
tightly related

Assessing market relatedness

Customers in adjacent markets base their buying decision on similar values, buy from the same sales channels and reference each other when making a buying decision.

To understand the level of relatedness between the customers in your primary market and the customers of your potential Backup/ Growth Option, think about the following questions:

To what extent do the customers share . . .

 Values and benefits?
(i.e., you can leverage your brand and reputation from one market to the other)

 Sales channels?
(i.e., you can utilise the same distribution channels for both markets)

 Word of mouth?
(i.e., satisfied customers in one market can promote your product in the other)

Once again, the overall market relatedness can then be rated as one of three levels:

Customers hardly share
not related

Customers share a little
somewhat related

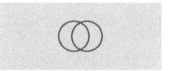

Customers share a lot
tightly related

Use the designated space in Worksheet 3 to assess the relatedness of possible Backup/ Growth Options to your Primary Market Opportunity.

The Bowling Pin Model by Geoffrey Moore

In his books 'Crossing the Chasm' and 'Inside the Tornado', which describe the diffusion of highly innovative products, Moore offers a model for crossing the chasm between the early and the main market by attacking one niche after the other. He terms this the 'Bowling Pin Strategy', as knocking over one target segment will help to knock over an adjacent niche, and thus lead to market expansion. In his model, adjacencies are based on leveraging the 'whole product' (i.e., offering related products to different customers) or on leveraging customers' references (i.e., offering different products to related customers).°

This is similar to our notions of product relatedness and market relatedness. In essence, Moore's subsequent niches serve a similar purpose as our Growth Options do: leveraging current resources and capabilities to enhance the economic gains of the firm.

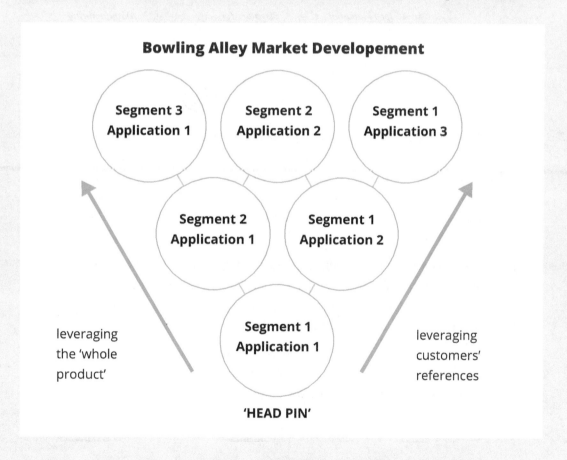

Bowling Alley Market Developement

Segment 3 Application 1

Segment 2 Application 2

Segment 1 Application 3

Segment 2 Application 1

Segment 1 Application 2

leveraging the 'whole product'

Segment 1 Application 1

leveraging customers' references

'HEAD PIN'

° To find out more take a look at: Crossing the Chasm/ Geoffrey Moore (1991);
Inside the Tornado/ Geoffrey Moore (1995)

Once the Primary Market Opportunity for Augury was chosen, it was time to think about their options portfolio and design their Agile Focus Strategy. The manufacturing machines market was an attractive candidate to examine. Cars and white appliances seemed too far out for now, and cooling containers did not seem to be a valuable enough opportunity.

However, once focused on the HVAC market for commercial buildings, two additional opportunities required further attention: elevators in commercial buildings and HVAC systems in residential buildings. These opportunities were clearly related to the firm's primary focus (just as Geoffrey Moore suggested in his Bowling Pin Model) and thus could be suitable to serve as Growth or as Backup Options.

	HVAC for residential buildings			Elevators for commercial buildings			Manufacturing machines		
Product Relatedness	∞	⊘⊘	**⊙⊙**	∞	**⊙⊙**	⊘⊘	∞	**⊙⊙**	⊘⊘
Market Relatedness	∞	**⊙⊙**	⊘⊘	∞	⊘⊘	**⊙⊙**	∞	**⊙⊙**	⊘⊘

Monitoring HVAC systems in residential buildings required a very similar solution to monitoring HVAC in commercial areas. Although the product would have to be cheaper, product relatedness is quite high. However, the markets were only somewhat related as residential houses do not necessarily rely on the same service providers, so word-of-mouth and marketing will definitely require additional effort.

Elevators for commercial buildings were just the opposite: the product shared some similarities but also required additional abilities as it will need to comply with specific regulations. Yet, the markets were tightly related because it would be the same users who would use both products.

As for manufacturing machines, these were only somewhat related on both aspects. Once this was understood, it became more apparent which opportunities can serve for future growth and which are suitable as backups for future redirection, if necessary.

AUGURY

Which market opportunities are suitable as Backup Options?

Backup Options are your 'Plan B'. They allow you to change direction if you find out that your initial opportunity isn't satisfying.
Eric Ries uses the term pivot to describe such redirection, referring to a shift in strategy that is accomplished by keeping one foot in place, as you shift the other in a new direction.°

This implies an attempt to leverage your knowledge and capabilities as much as possible once a strategic shift is required. Hence, Backup Options are attractive opportunities that should be as related as possible to your Primary Market Opportunity. However, as these will constitute your Plan B, Backup Options should not share the same major risks with your Primary Market Opportunity or rely on the same major assumptions. In short: you want to be able to succeed with them, even though you have failed in pursuing your primary opportunity!

Use the Attractiveness Map and the evaluations you have done in Worksheet 2 to think about the major risks and potential show stoppers associated with your Primary Market Opportunity and compare them to those of your other options. For example, if success in your primary market depends heavily on regulation, find a Backup Option that does not depend on such regulation.

Remember that it is extremely important to become familiar with the weaknesses and major risks of your primary market, as you're much less likely to be caught off-guard that way. Balancing these pitfalls by keeping an appropriate Backup Option open will help you manage this risk with minimum effort.

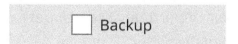

Mark whether your opportunities are suitable to become Backup Options in the designated spot of Worksheet 3.

° To find out more take a look at: The Lean Startup/ Eric Ries (2011)

Which market opportunities are suitable as Growth Options?

Growth Options allow you to increase your value creation potential. You can pursue them in parallel to your Primary Market Opportunity if the potential that the latter offers is not sufficient – or simply keep them open to be pursued in the future, if you desire to do so.

In any case, you are looking for options that should be as attractive as possible (i.e., with high Potential and low Challenge) and that will be as closely related to your primary opportunity, so that pursuing them will require limited additional effort. Think about your Growth Options as your strategic roadmap to success. If you choose, for example, a Quick Win opportunity as your initial target, you can set a Moon Shot opportunity as your Growth Option.

For example, Tesla's affordable electric vehicle for the mass market was a clear Growth Option, when Elon Musk (Tesla's co-founder and CEO) decided to focus initially on the luxury sports car market.

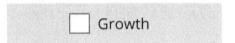

Growth

Examine your opportunities and mark whether one or more are suitable to become your Growth Option(s) in the designated spot of Worksheet 3.

> *Sometimes, an opportunity can serve as your Backup Option and also as your Growth Option. If your Market Opportunity Set includes an attractive opportunity that is highly related to your Primary Market Opportunity but does not share the same major risks with it, this might be the case for you. In this situation, you will most likely not need to keep two different options open.*

For Augury, it became apparent that the residential HVAC option and the elevators for commercial buildings option can be good Growth Options once they are successful in pursuing their Primary Market Opportunity (HVAC for commercial buildings).

Yet, the main risk of this Primary Market Opportunity was that the value of the solution will not be clear enough to the customers, as they will first have to be educated about the product and its performance benefits.

If this would eventually hinder success, Augury could change direction and offer predictive maintenance solutions for manufacturing machines, where their value is more critical. Manufacturing machines can therefore serve as a Backup Option for Augury.

HVAC for commercial buildings

	HVAC for residential buildings	Elevators for commercial buildings	Manufacturing machines
Product Relatedness	◯◯ ◯◯ **⦿⦿**	◯◯ **⦿⦿** ◯◯	◯◯ **⦿⦿** ◯◯
Market Relatedness	◯◯ **⦿⦿** ◯◯	◯◯ ◯◯ **⦿⦿**	◯◯ **⦿⦿** ◯◯
Backup Option	☐ Backup	☐ Backup	☑ Backup
Growth Option	☑ Growth	☑ Growth	☐ Growth

Remember that some opportunities can serve as Backup and as Growth Options both at the same time. KalOptics provides one such example.

The firm decided to initially focus on film producers striving to create complicated visual effects. Animation producers look up to film producers when making their buying decision and require a relatively similar product. Hence, they are a natural candidate for a Growth Option.

The market for designers and the market for advertisers, however, require a simpler product and are not strongly influenced by the film industry. They do not share the technological risk of capturing real-life or moving objects, and success will likely not be hindered by low adoption rates in the primary market. Hence, both opportunities can serve as Growth or as Backup Options.

KalOptics' Growth and Backup Options provide the basis for their market roll-out plan, combined with the ability to contain risk, if things don't play out as planned.

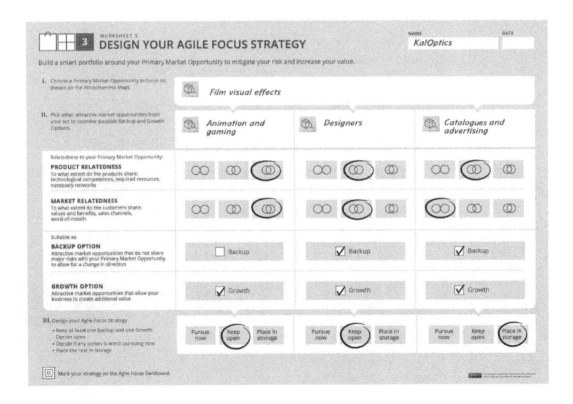

Step 3: Determining your Agile Focus Strategy

Now that you have chosen your Primary Market Opportunity, and have assessed several Backup and Growth Options, it is time to finalise your Agile Focus Strategy. Two decisions are still required:

☐ Which of the assessed market opportunities will eventually serve as your Backup Option and as your Growth Option?

☐ How much effort are you planning to invest in these options in the near future?

Once you make these decisions, you will be able to determine which market opportunities will you:

Pursue now

Keep open for later

Place in storage

> *Combining all of these important considerations will enable you to do exactly what the Agile Focus Strategy is all about:*
> *focus on the most attractive market opportunity while maintaining your agility and manoeuvrability.*

133

Choosing your Backup Options and your Growth Options

In order to design a compelling and promising Agile Focus Strategy, pick at least one Backup Option and one Growth Option. It will help you tremendously to prepare for an uncertain future!

If you have several alternatives that can serve as your Growth Option or as your Backup Option, choose the ones that you believe will best fit the bill. While it is possible to keep several options open, it comes with the price tag of spreading your attention and your resources. In effect, although keeping an option open requires little investment, keeping too many options open can easily become too large an effort for a small venture and strain the bandwidth that you and your team members have.

If you have several candidates, choosing your Backup and your Growth Options may not be straightforward due to two widespread trade-offs:

Attractiveness vs. relatedness

Some options can be more attractive (i.e., with high Potential and low Challenge), but less related to your primary opportunity, or vice versa. In this case, the benefits of high attractiveness oppose the costs of low relatedness.

Relatedness vs. risk balancing

Highly related options usually tend to share similar risks, while distant options offer dispersed risk. Therefore, options that are less related to your Primary Market Opportunity can often better balance its major risks.

Be aware of these trade-offs so that you can make an informed choice.

Investing in your Backup and your Growth Options

The Agile Focus Strategy, which is built on real options reasoning, suggests that you keep your Backup and Growth Options open. You will be better prepared to pursue them later on, if conditions become more favourable.

Keeping your options open

In general, keeping an option open means that you allocate little resources and management attention to this opportunity. You should keep it 'breathing', and make sure that you do not lock yourself out of this path. Here is how you do that:

Stay informed

First and foremost, you need to allocate some resources and attention to staying informed about this particular market: What's going on? Are there new trends? New products? New entrants? etc. You can do this by following relevant market researches or industry reports, visiting tradeshows or keeping good contacts with key people in that market. The idea is to keep your finger on the pulse in order to maintain and advance your understanding of the market.

Build flexible resources and capabilities

Second, because you have identified options for backup or for growth early on, you now have the possibility to develop your resources and capabilities in a way that allows for greater flexibility and robustness. Instead of locking yourself into one particular path, develop your resources and capabilities so that they can be adapted with minimal effort.

For example, sometimes you can overcome a technological challenge by developing a solution that is tailored to your specific offering but will not be suitable for other options. In such a case, it is worthwhile to spend the extra effort to develop a broader solution, one that can also serve as the basis for your future options. Intellectual property is another example. When you file your patents, make sure that your future options are reflected in your claims.

Develop an appropriate identity

Organisational identity is an important yet sometimes overlooked aspect in new venture creation. It relates to how employees, as well as customers and investors, perceive the firm and provides an answer to questions such as: 'Who are we?' 'What are we doing?' 'What do we want to be in the future?'. The identity statement defines what is important and essential to the organisation, and usually includes organisational ideology, management philosophy and culture.°

Identity is enduring and difficult to change. Therefore, open options must be taken into consideration when managers develop their organisational identity and define their branding.

Keeping selected options open does not endanger your ability to focus on your primary market because it requires minimal attention.

Think of resource allocation as a continuum that runs from 'none' to 'many': keeping an option open is somewhere above zero and usually requires about 5%–10% of your time and attention.

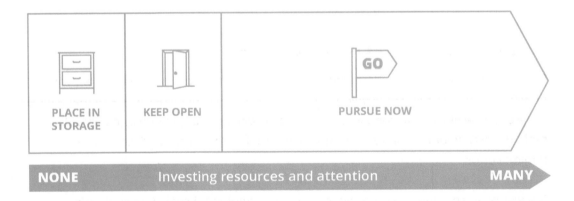

You can also decide to invest more than just a few resources for keeping your options open. This is especially relevant for your Growth Option, which you may actually decide to pursue right now, in parallel with your Primary Market Opportunity.

° To find out more take a look at: Organizational identity/ Albert and Whetten (1985)

Pursue options now – in parallel

Executing your Growth Option in parallel with your Primary Market Opportunity means that you allocate your resources and attention to pursue both markets simultaneously and to develop the required skills and expertise for succeeding in both.

This endeavour is challenging for a small venture due to the scarce human and financial capital. Management attention and time are always limited and may simply be spread too thinly. However, in some cases such a parallel strategy may be beneficial and can lead to improved results.

Q Research insights

In one of our research studies, we examined the strategy of over 300 new technology ventures and their performance at the age of 3 years.

We wanted to understand under which conditions, if any, pursuing more than one market opportunity in parallel yields better performance despite the resource limitations of new start-ups.

Our results showed that the parallel strategy led to superior performance when market uncertainty was very high, that is, when founders operated in a new market in which customer needs could not be clearly articulated and easily translated into products. Start-ups that adopted a parallel strategy under such conditions outperformed start-ups that pursued one single market opportunity at a time.[o]

---

[o] To find out more take a look at: Experimentation, uncertainty, and the performance of new technology ventures/ Tal, Gruber & de Haan (Dissertation Technion)

Two major considerations should guide your decision of whether to keep your option open for later or to pursue it now in parallel with your Primary Market Opportunity:

1 How critical is this option to your venture's performance? If your Primary Market Opportunity is highly uncertain and very risky, or if its value creation potential is not satisfying enough, you can increase your gains and lower your risk by pursuing a parallel strategy.

2 How related is this option to your Primary Market Opportunity? Because pursuing opportunities simultaneously requires a lot of effort and attention, a parallel strategy tends to be feasible only when options are highly related, because this will allow you to leverage your resources and capabilities.

As an example for such a parallel strategy, consider Camero – a world leading provider and pioneer of through-wall-imaging solutions. Camero's products provide real-time observation of stationary and moving objects concealed behind walls or barriers. This revolutionary solution is suitable for intelligence and tactical applications – needed by both military troops and law enforcement officers. While both markets had large potential, the main challenges lie in accessing these customers and in bearing the very long and complex sales process.

To balance this risk, Camero's managers decided to pursue these two markets simultaneously: military and police. The products they required were similar, and the markets were tightly related, as they were both leaning on government budgets and sharing the same values and word-of-mouth. This tight relatedness enabled Camero to pursue such a parallel strategy, to increase their value and mitigate their risk with minimum effort.

At the end of this process, it should be clear to you which market opportunities will serve as your Backup Options and as your Growth Options, and how much effort you are planning to invest in each: Will you invest much effort to fully pursue them now – in parallel with your Primary Market Opportunity – or will you invest little effort to consciously keep them open?

What about all the other market opportunities?

Your Agile Focus Strategy is already taking shape. But there is one more element to discuss: What about all the other market opportunities that you had evaluated but did not select as your Primary Market Opportunity or your Backup/ Growth Options?

Do not discard them, but rather place them in 'storage' for now – they might become valuable options in the future!

Storing market opportunities

Placing a market opportunity in 'storage' means that you do nothing about it, for now.

You only keep it in the back of your mind. On the 'resource allocation' continuum described before, stored options are located at the far left, as they require no effort or management attention.

For instance, options that are suitable for storage may be those that are currently too far out – either because they are completely distant from the direction that you chose, or because their time has just not come yet.

These options can become relevant someday, either for you to pursue or for licensing to others. Luckily, you do not need to pay storage rent, so market opportunities can be stored as long as you wish.

At the bottom of Worksheet 3, you can indicate your final decision: Which of the options will you pursue now? Keep open for later? Or place in storage?

Congratulations

You are now ready to depict your strategy on the Agile Focus Dartboard!

As Augury were embarking on their very first steps in their market domain, they consciously decided to keep both of their Growth Options open as well as their Backup Option.

They figured that as they get more acquainted with commercial building managers and service providers, they will be able to better assess these options over time. So, when the time comes, they would be ready for adaptation or change.

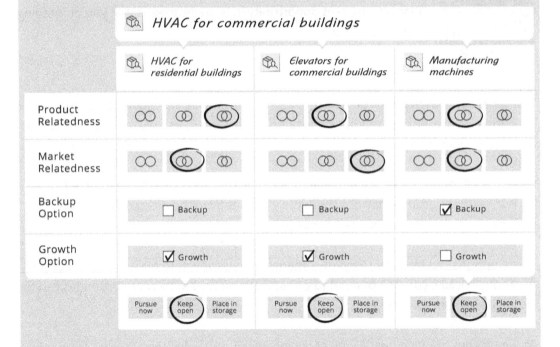

They also decided to place in storage all the other market opportunities that they had in their set, as they were currently too far out from their chosen direction.

The outcome – your Agile Focus Dartboard

You are now ready to depict your Agile Focus Strategy on the Market Opportunity Navigator. Use the Dartboard to mark your Primary Market Opportunity, the options that you keep open for backup or for growth and the options that you place in storage.

> *If you decide to pursue two options in parallel, put them both at the centre of your Dartboard!*

The Agile Focus Dartboard allows you to depict your strategy and to discuss it with team members, employees and other stakeholders. It has many implications for how you build and develop your venture. These implications will be discussed in detail in the next chapter.

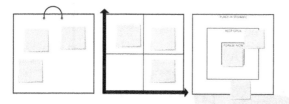

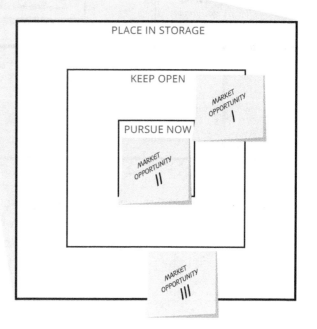

Finally, Augury's Agile Focus Strategy was set: they will focus on the HVAC market for commercial buildings, they will keep open one Backup Option (manufacturing machines) and two Growth Options (residential HVAC and elevators), and they will currently put aside all other market opportunities.

Their strategy can now be depicted on the Agile Focus Dartboard:

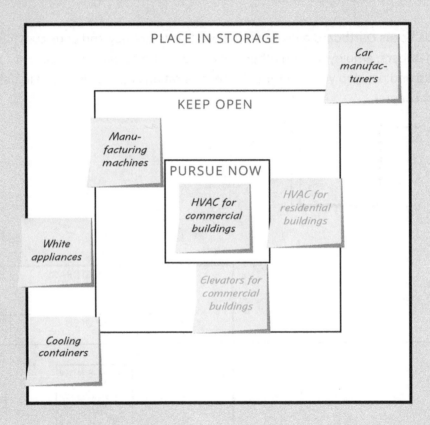

Note that the two Growth Options are marked in a different colour – simply to signal in a visual manner that these are new market opportunities that have not yet been assessed. They were also added to the Market Opportunity Set, but still need to be positioned on the Attractiveness Map.

As the Navigator is designed to be a dynamic tool, it is perfectly fine to add or dismiss options as you move forward with your learning and build your understanding.

The founders of KalOptics also depicted their Agile Focus Strategy on the Dartboard. They not only decided on what would be their Primary Market Opportunity and which options they will keep open but also planned their market development roll-out: beginning with the film studios, then growing to the animation and gaming market and then to the designer market. The market for catalogues and advertisers was placed in storage for the time being.

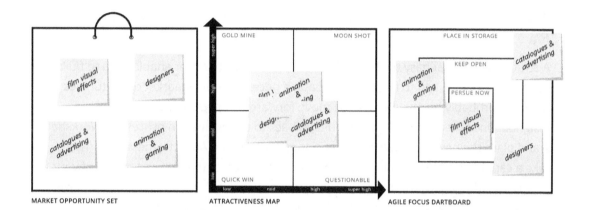

MARKET OPPORTUNITY SET   ATTRACTIVENESS MAP   AGILE FOCUS DARTBOARD

? FAQs

How can we make sure that Agile Focusing doesn't lead us to de-focusing?

Many entrepreneurs that we have worked with described the fine line between staying focused and feeling scattered. With the Agile Focus Strategy, you deliberately plan your focus to be a bit broader, so that you increase your agility. However, you clearly define and state your focused strategy at the end of this process, so that you do not have to worry about losing your way. Remember that the most difficult part in focusing is deciding what not to do, a question for which the Agile Focus Strategy provides a clear answer.

What shall we do if we discover additional market opportunities after we have already set our strategy?

A strategy is not that easy to change. Yet, the Agile Focus mindset enables you to build cognitive flexibility, and to be ready to adapt, if necessary. New market opportunities will most probably be revealed as you move forward, get exposure and acquire new insights. Once that happens, you should go back to the evaluation process of Worksheet 2 and place the newly identified market opportunity on the Attractiveness Map. Then, take a careful look to determine if this opportunity deserves (partial) adaptation of your strategy – either as your primary market or as your Backup/ Growth Option. The Navigator provides an effective learning companion that helps you to deal smartly with new developments – on one hand, not to jump too quickly on a new wagon and on the other hand to be open for change and adaptation if it would improve your situation.

Investors usually fund start-ups only if they believe that they focus on one target. Is the Agile Focus Strategy relevant at all for finding investment?

It is true that investors, and especially VCs, hedge their bets by investing in several firms and will most likely invest in your firm only if they find your Primary Market Opportunity interesting enough. However, investors do understand the importance of agility and will be happy to learn that you have other attractive options in your pipeline, and that you know how to prepare your venture for adaptation. Additionally, investors want to see that you have a well-defined strategy. Hesitating between potential market opportunities will turn them off. Use the Navigator to communicate your strategy in a clear manner, and to convey the logic behind your strategic decisions.

Let's recap with flying robots

To recap on how you should apply the Navigator and turn a complex strategic choice into a structured decision-making process, let's look at Flyability.

Flyability is a Swiss start-up – a spin-off from the Swiss Federal Institute of Technology (EPFL) in Lausanne – that is developing a collision-tolerant flying robot. This drone is unique as it can fly in complex and confined spaces and in contact with humans, because it has a surrounding cage that protects it.

Well . . . where should this drone be applied?

The answer is definitely dazzling, because there are numerous options. That is exactly where the Market Opportunity Navigator comes in handy.

Step 1: Generating a Market Opportunity Set

To begin with, let's understand Flyability's core technology. The drone that they plan to develop has unique accessibility due to the decoupled and light protection cage that surrounds it. It can fly or roll on any surface and will actually be able to operate in a range of temperatures (from 0°C to around 50°C). It will be piloted manually with an on-site video screen, even in very dark, smoked or dusty environments, but only for a limited duration due to battery limitations. Lastly, it carries an automated, fully adjustable imagery system, with HD and thermal recordings that are live streamed to the control screen and recorded for a later analysis.

Flyability's unique drones will therefore be able to inspect and explore inaccessible places – regardless of how complex and confined they are, thus avoiding the need to send humans into dangerous environments. These unique abilities can be utilised for many different applications, including inspections, surveillance, deliveries or entertainment – to name but a few.

At its early stage, the team identified several promising applications that could bring real value from the start: inspection of complex industry machineries, inspection of difficult-to-maintain infrastructures, and also security or search and rescue applications. As detailed in Worksheet 1, these applications can serve many types of customers.

After an initial rough screening, Flyability's team decides to further examine those market opportunities that seem to be more reachable and especially those that mainly require indoor navigation (to suit the expected initial limitations of the drone).

Their Market Opportunity Set includes five options: inspection of boilers and heaters in thermal power plants, inspection of rooms in nuclear power plants, inspection of storage tanks in the oil and gas industry, vessel inspection in the maritime industry and, lastly, intelligence and surveillance for police forces.

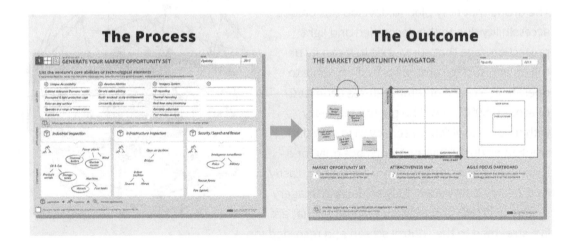

Step 2: Evaluating the attractiveness of market opportunities

The Flyability team is now ready for the next step. By using Worksheet 2, they can evaluate each of these market opportunities and place them on the Attractiveness Map.

 ## Opportunity 1:
Inspection of boilers and heaters in thermal power plants

Plants converting heat energy into electric power operate under extreme temperatures with huge boilers and super-heaters. These facilities have to be inspected periodically, which means that individuals have to work at great heights and gain access either with ropes, sky climbers or scaffolding. One can easily imagine that implementing the required safety measures, bringing in and installing the inspection equipment, and performing the inspection manually are lengthy processes that result in several days of costly shutdowns . . . and they expose workers to great risks! Thus, the ability to replace a manned intervention with a collision-tolerant drone can bring significant value to these energy plants, as they would be able to save time and cost, and increase safety.

Here is how Flyability's team evaluated this market opportunity:

Potential	Challenge
The unique value that this drone can bring creates a 'super-high' compelling reason to buy. The market size itself is high (there are about 100000 plants worldwide), and so is the economic viability, due to large margins and customers' ability to pay.	The firm already had the know-how for developing the drone and estimated both the implementation obstacles and the time to revenue as 'mid', taking into account the distribution requirements and the length of a sale cycle. The external risks seemed low, because competition is limited and success is not dependent on other parties.
The overall potential is 'high'.	**The overall challenge is 'low-mid'.**

Overall, this is an attractive market opportunity, located in the Gold Mine quarter of the Attractiveness Map.

Opportunity 2:
Inspection of rooms in nuclear power plants

Another market opportunity is the periodic inspection of the immediate environment to nuclear reactors, which is an activity that involves challenging work in an extremely hazardous environment. The operators of nuclear reactors thus have a strong interest in adopting any good solution that could replace manned interventions in radioactive areas.

This is how Flyability's team evaluated the Potential and the Challenge associated with this market opportunity:

Potential	Challenge
While the compelling reason to buy and the economic viability of this market are 'super high', the market volume is relatively low, as there are around 450 nuclear reactors worldwide.	Because the effect of radioactiveness is unknown, the implementation obstacles seem 'super high'. Time to revenue is estimated as 'mid' and coupled with relatively high external risks due to competitive threats and adoption barriers.
The overall potential is 'mid-high'.	**The overall challenge is 'high'.**

Overall, this market opportunity is located between the Moon Shot and the Questionable quarters of the Attractiveness Map.

Opportunity 3:
Inspection of storage tanks in the oil and gas industry

Every few years, oil and gas producers have to perform a thorough inspection of their huge storage tanks – a procedure that includes a visual inspection of fire protection piping, overfill protection, roof inspection and more. To perform their demanding work, the inspectors have to enter the huge tanks and work at great heights in pitch-dark conditions! Usual methods such as scaffolding or rope access are costly and time-consuming. By employing a collision-tolerant drone, oil and gas producers could generate significant savings in time and cost, and increase safety.

Here is a summary of how Flyability's team evaluated this market opportunity:

Potential	Challenge
The value that this drone can bring creates a 'super-high' compelling reason to buy. While the market size itself is rated as 'mid' (because inspections are mainly done by specialised inspection companies), the economic potential is still high due to large margins and customers' ability to pay.	The major challenge of this market is the need to comply with regulations for working in explosive environments. This implies relatively 'high' implementation obstacles and 'mid-high' time to revenue. The external risks were also estimated as 'mid-high', as conventional drones can do part of the job in large tanks.
The overall potential is 'high'.	**The overall challenge is 'high'.**

Overall, this market opportunity is located in the Moon Shot quarter of the Attractiveness Map.

 ### Opportunity 4:
Vessel inspection in the maritime industry

Vessels have to be inspected once every 5 years to maintain their permit. These inspections are done by specific classification companies that are dedicated to safe ships and clean seas. Examinations are done in deep, dark and confined areas of the boat, as well as in open air platforms and large tanks. Just as before, replacing a manned intervention with a collision-tolerant drone can bring significant value to these customers, allowing important savings in time and cost, and increased safety.

Flyability's team evaluated this market opportunity in the following way:

Potential	Challenge
Although the compelling reason to buy is 'super high', and so is the economic viability, this is a relatively low volume market as there is a very limited number of classification companies worldwide.	Because this market requires high levels of navigation stability, the implementation obstacles were rated as 'mid-high'. Distribution and sales are relatively simple and short, so time to revenue seems to be 'mid'. External risks were rated as 'mid-high', especially due to dependencies on industry standards and regulations.
The overall potential is 'mid-high'.	**The overall challenge is 'mid-high'.**

Overall, this market opportunity is located right in the middle of the Attractiveness Map – with no clear location in any quarter.

 ### Opportunity 5:
Intelligence and surveillance for police forces

A drone that can safely fly near walls and humans may be extremely valuable for security purposes, and especially for intelligence, surveillance and indoor reconnaissance. Police units, fighting against crime and terrorism, could use the images from the drone to increase the success of their operation and the personal safety of their professionals.

Flyability's team evaluated this market opportunity in the following manner:

Potential

The drone can provide an effective solution to a real unmet need – thus, the compelling reason to buy is high. While the market volume is 'super high', the economic viability was estimated as 'mid', especially since customers' ability to pay and to generate high margins is questionable.

The overall potential is 'high'.

Challenge

Product has to be very stable and very quiet, and entering the police procurement channels is challenging. Hence implementation obstacles seem high. The long sale cycle and the long training period may lead to a 'super-high' time to revenue, and so are the external risks due to high competitive threat and dependencies on third parties, and very high barriers for adoption.

The overall challenge is 'super high'.

Overall, this market opportunity is located in the Moon Shot quarter of the Attractiveness Map.

Once the evaluation was completed, the Flyability team was able to depict these five market opportunities on the Attractiveness Map and to visually evaluate and compare their attractiveness.

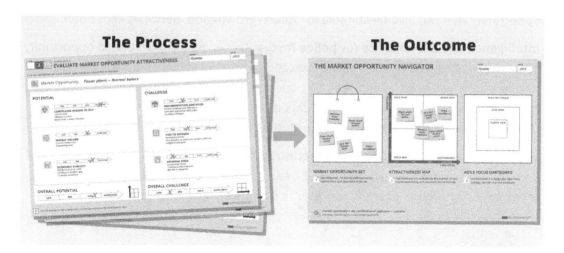

Step 3: Designing the Agile Focus Strategy

Next, Flyability's team can use Worksheet 3 to design its Agile Focus Strategy and depict it on the Dartboard.

Examining the Attractiveness Map shows that **inspecting boilers and heaters in thermal power plants** is the most attractive market opportunity for Flyability at this stage. It offers a clear value proposition to a large-volume market and encounters the least amount of challenge for becoming successful. Hence, the team decided that this will be the venture's Primary Market Opportunity.

Once set, it is time to design a smart portfolio of Backup and Growth Options that will allow Flyability to mitigate risks and increase the value of its activities. Three market opportunities are relevant candidates:

Inspection of storage tanks in the oil and gas industry: While the product is only somewhat related (as it requires the ability to work in explosive areas), the markets are relatively close, especially since they share the same distribution channels for non-destructive testing equipment. Overall, this opportunity is suitable for future growth and, hence, is kept open.

Inspection of vessels in the maritime industry: Although some stability improvements are required, the product is tightly related. Yet, the customer segments only share a limited number of similarities. Overall, this is quite an attractive opportunity that can also be suitable for future growth and, hence, is kept open.

Intelligence and surveillance for police forces: This is the most unrelated opportunity. While the product shares some similarities, the customer segments are completely distant: customers don't value the same benefits and don't share sales channels or word-of-mouth. In general, this opportunity bears different risks from that of the primary market and, hence, qualifies as a Backup Option. Flyability will keep it open.

The last examined opportunity – **inspection of rooms in nuclear power plants** – will be placed in storage for now. Because it bears unique challenges in complying with radioactive environments and it represents a relatively low-volume market, it is the least attractive option.

Flyability's Agile Focus Strategy is now set and can be depicted on the Dartboard.

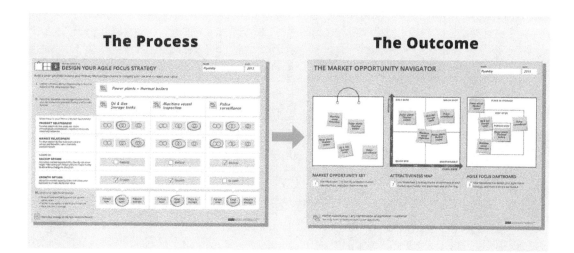

This strategic choice provides a clear market entry roadmap and a clear technological roadmap for Flyability's managers. It enables them to set the right development priorities, build relevant networks and design the proper marketing materials. Moreover, the team has now the right skills for applying a well-structured decision making process whenever it is time to rethink their strategy.

Taking everything together, here are the full worksheets and the Navigator's main design board for Flyability.

Worksheet 1

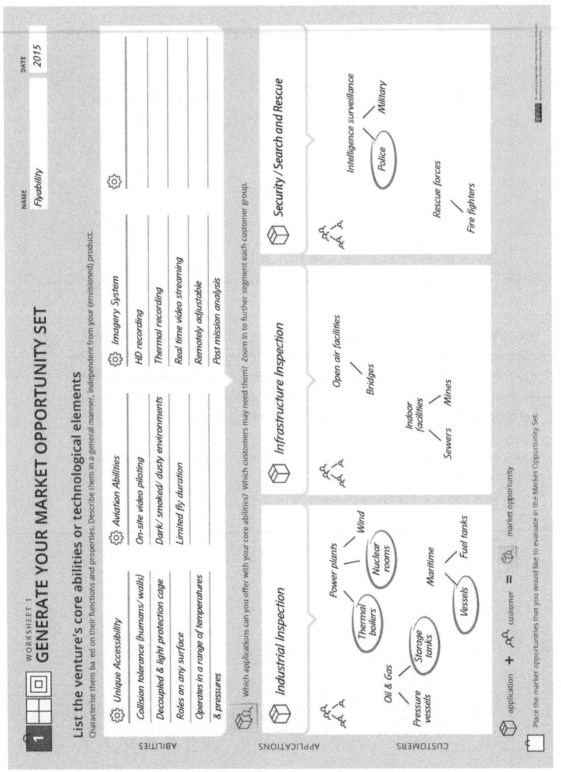

WORKSHEET 1
GENERATE YOUR MARKET OPPORTUNITY SET

NAME: Flyability
DATE: 2015

List the venture's core abilities or technological elements

Characterise them based on their functions and properties. Describe them in a general manner, independent from your (envisioned) product.

ABILITIES

⚙ Unique Accessibility
- Collision tolerance (humans/ walls)
- Decoupled & light protection cage
- Roles on any surface
- Operates in a range of temperatures & pressures

⚙ Aviation Abilities
- On-site video piloting
- Dark/ smoked/ dusty environments
- Limited fly duration

⚙ Imagery System
- HD recording
- Thermal recording
- Real time video streaming
- Remotely adjustable
- Post mission analysis

⚙

Which applications can you offer with your core abilities? Which customers may need them? Zoom in to further segment each customer group.

APPLICATIONS

◇ Industrial Inspection

◇ Infrastructure Inspection

◇ Security / Search and Rescue

CUSTOMERS

Industrial Inspection:
- Power plants
  - Wind
  - Nuclear rooms
  - Thermal boilers
- Oil & Gas
  - Storage tanks
  - Pressure vessels
- Maritime
  - Vessels
  - Fuel tanks

Infrastructure Inspection:
- Open air facilities
  - Bridges
- Indoor facilities
  - Sewers
  - Mines

Security / Search and Rescue:
- Intelligence surveillance
  - Police
  - Military
- Rescue forces
  - Fire fighters

application + ⚕ customer = ◇ market opportunity

Place the market opportunities that you would like to evaluate in the Market Opportunity Set.

Worksheet 2 (for one market opportunity)

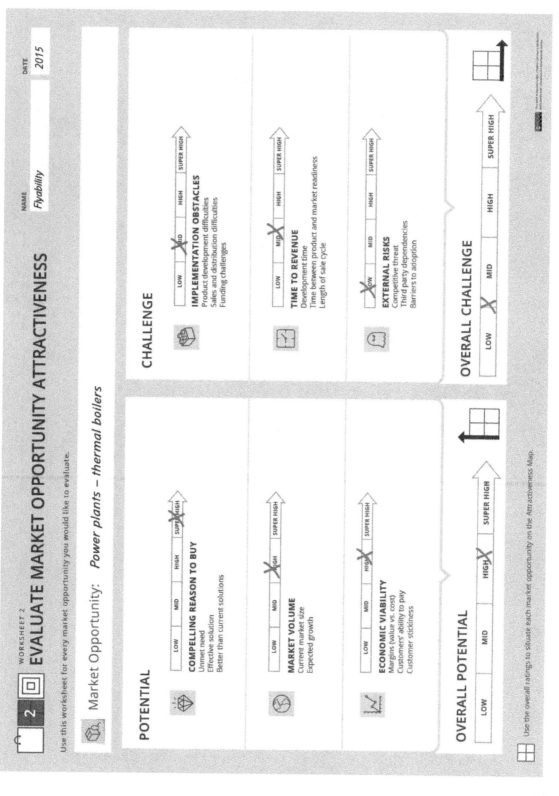

WORKSHEET 2

EVALUATE MARKET OPPORTUNITY ATTRACTIVENESS

NAME *Flyability*

DATE 2015

Use this worksheet for every market opportunity you would like to evaluate.

Market Opportunity: *Power plants – thermal boilers*

POTENTIAL

COMPELLING REASON TO BUY
Unmet need
Effective solution
Better than current solutions

LOW — MID — HIGH — SUPER HIGH

MARKET VOLUME
Current market size
Expected growth

LOW — MID — HIGH — SUPER HIGH

ECONOMIC VIABILITY
Margins (value vs. cost)
Customers' ability to pay
Customer stickiness

LOW — MID — HIGH — SUPER HIGH

OVERALL POTENTIAL

LOW — MID — HIGH — SUPER HIGH

CHALLENGE

IMPLEMENTATION OBSTACLES
Product development difficulties
Sales and distribution difficulties
Funding challenges

LOW — MID — HIGH — SUPER HIGH

TIME TO REVENUE
Development time
Time between product and market readiness
Length of sale cycle

LOW — MID — HIGH — SUPER HIGH

EXTERNAL RISKS
Competitive threat
Third party dependencies
Barriers to adoption

LOW — MID — HIGH — SUPER HIGH

OVERALL CHALLENGE

LOW — MID — HIGH — SUPER HIGH

Use the overall ratings to situate each market opportunity on the Attractiveness Map.

Worksheet 3

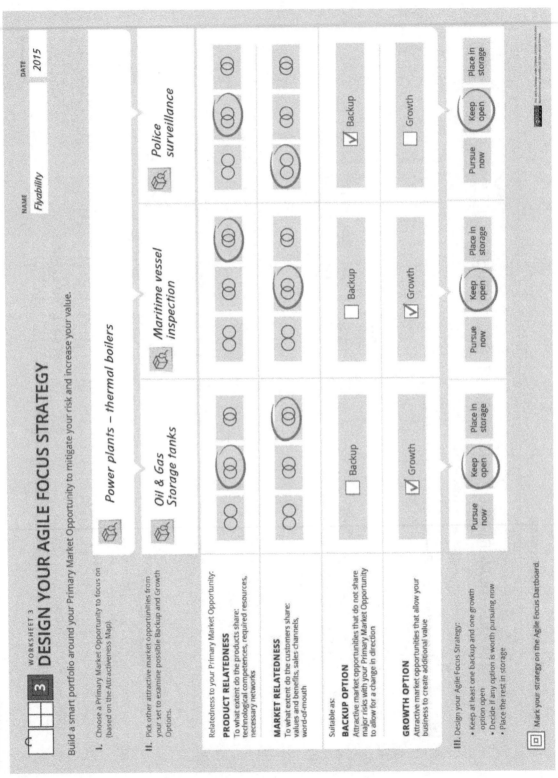

3 DESIGN YOUR AGILE FOCUS STRATEGY

NAME Flyability

DATE 2015

Build a smart portfolio around your Primary Market Opportunity to mitigate your risk and increase your value.

I. Choose a Primary Market Opportunity to focus on (based on the Attractiveness Map).

II. Pick other attractive market opportunities from your set to examine possible Backup and Growth Options.

Relatedness to your Primary Market Opportunity:

PRODUCT RELATEDNESS
To what extent do the products share: technological competences, required resources, necessary networks

MARKET RELATEDNESS
To what extent do the customers share: values and benefits, sales channels, word-of-mouth

Suitable as:

BACKUP OPTION
Attractive market opportunities that do not share major risks with your Primary Market Opportunity to allow for a change in direction

GROWTH OPTION
Attractive market opportunities that allow your business to create additional value

III. Design your Agile Focus Strategy:
• Keep at least one backup and one growth option open
• Decide if any option is worth pursuing now
• Place the rest in storage

Mark your strategy on the Agile Focus Dartboard.

Power plants – thermal boilers

Oil & Gas Storage tanks

Maritime vessel inspection

Police surveillance

156

The Navigator

THE MARKET OPPORTUNITY NAVIGATOR

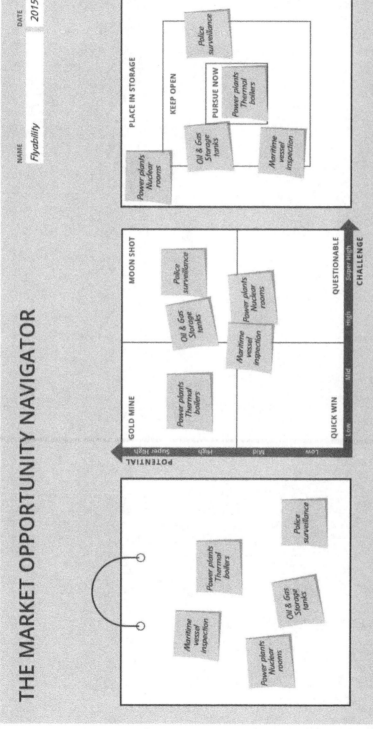

MARKET OPPORTUNITY SET

1   Use Worksheet 1 to identify potential market opportunities, and place them in the set

ATTRACTIVENESS MAP

2   Use Worksheet 2 to evaluate the attractiveness of each market opportunity, and place each one on the map

AGILE FOCUS DARTBOARD

3   Use Worksheet 3 to design your Agile Focus Strategy, and mark it on the Dartboard

market opportunity = any combination of application + customer
Use sticky notes to represent each market opportunity

3

Implications and additional benefits

The Market Opportunity Navigator is your business tool to successfully navigate the market opportunity landscape, whenever this is required.

In order to work effectively with the Market Opportunity Navigator, it is important to:

- Understand how the Agile Focus Strategy influences key issues in venture creation and in commercialising innovations

- Learn how you can benefit from the Market Opportunity Navigator over time

- Employ it in concert with other business tools

3.1 Implications of the Agile Focus Strategy

The final outcome of the Market Opportunity Navigator is your Agile Focus Strategy. It shows how you can navigate smartly on the market opportunity landscape: you can focus on the most attractive opportunity and maintain your agility while doing so. In effect, by deliberately keeping open your Backup and Growth Options, you enhance not only the agility of your resources and capabilities but also your cognitive flexibility . . . and that of your management team, your employees and your stakeholders.

In short, the Agile Focus Strategy has important implications for many areas and activities associated with your commercialisation effort.

Think about the . . .

▫ Resources and capabilities that you will continue to develop and build over time

▫ Identity, culture and structure of your venture

▫ Branding and marketing you will employ in your commercialisation efforts

▫ Fundraising efforts you will engage in

Resources and capabilities over time: developing agility and acting with foresight!

The Dartboard provides an overview of the market opportunities that you can exploit – now, and over time. Having such an early understanding of the markets that can (potentially) be entered also helps you in taking key decisions regarding your resources and capabilities, and how you want to develop them over time. In essence, by having some foresight on this front, you will be able to develop your resources and capabilities in a way that will enable greater flexibility and agility – and these features are key when you should need to pivot to another market, or when you want to diversify to new markets!

Build a modular technology

Given that you know about future opportunities, you may want to build your technology in a modular manner so that you will be able to deploy it with greater flexibility – thereby saving time and money when pivoting or exploiting additional market opportunities! In any case, make sure that you do not lock yourself into one particular development path for your technological capabilities. Although at times it is tempting to tailor your technology in a way that allows you to cater to one specific market (because it may save you time and money in the short term), it will become fairly cumbersome, if not impossible, to adapt this technology to other applications. So, be very strict about this, and make sure that your R&D team is aligned with this guidance.

Cast a wider intellectual property (IP) net

Your Agile Focus Strategy should also influence your Intellectual Property (IP) strategy. Now that you know of additional market opportunities, you are able to proactively protect your invention in these domains. When you file your patents, make sure that your future options are reflected in your claims or application fields, to maximise your IP potential.

Take into consideration future human resource needs

You may also want to think about the people you will be hiring in a manner that takes into account your future market opportunities. Perhaps some employees bring the necessary skills to develop your technology in a more flexible manner or are better equipped for your sales and marketing efforts in current and future market domains? Furthermore, think of how you define their roles in the organisation, in a way that open-mindedness and agility are encouraged.

Build and involve your stakeholder network

Stakeholders have a key interest in the opportunities that you will (potentially) exploit. These could be your investors, your advisory board or other potential partners and allies. All these stakeholders need to be aware of your Agile Focus Strategy, and even more importantly, they may help you in its implementation. Hence, be smart about picking the right people in your network, with the relevant experience and attitude, so that they will not lock you out of your future option(s).

Medic Vision provides an illustration for this important point. As the firm decided to pivot from developing computer-aided diagnostic tools for brain scans to developing SafeCT (an add-on that enables low-dose CT imaging), they actually had to find new investors, as their current ones were locked on pursuing the original idea. Fortunately, Medic Vision succeeded in this strategic shift, but it was definitely painful and costly.

The identity of your venture, its culture and its structure

The market(s) a firm is serving is (are) not only of significance for creating value. Your choice of market opportunities also has a powerful influence on the DNA of your firm: 'what your firm is all about' and how others (potential employees, stakeholders, customers etc.) will perceive it. In fact, it is not only the market opportunities that you choose to pursue but also the scope of your focus that influence these profound characteristics.

Q **Research insights**

In a study that examined the emergence of 25 new technology ventures, we investigated how different types of market focus influence the organisational identity of these newly created firms.[o]

The results show that the founders' definition of 'who we are as an organisation' clearly depends on the scope of market opportunities that they intend to pursue:

☐ Ventures that adopt a 'laser-sharp' focus approach tend to develop a relatively narrow identity, which was mainly based on the specific product that they wanted to develop.

☐ Ventures that adopt an Agile Focus approach define their organisational identity in a fairly broad manner, often emphasising a wide market domain or a broadly defined need.

☐ Un-focused ventures (i.e., those that had not yet adopted a strategic focus) define their emerging firm in the widest possible manner, mainly based on the technology they develop.

In short, your Agile Focus Strategy will shape the identity of your firm and its culture. It will also affect how you design the structure of your company. Without a doubt, these are some of the most profound, far-reaching characteristics of your venture!

Imprinting the firm's identity

An identity statement defines what is important and essential to the venture, and usually draws on ideological ideas that are important to the founder and his or her plans for the venture. It relates to how employees, as well as customers and investors, perceive the firm, and provides an answer to questions such as: 'Who are we?' 'What are we doing?' 'What do we want to be in the future?'

---

o To find out more take a look at: Experimentation, uncertainty, and the performance of new technology ventures/ Tal, Gruber & de Haan (Dissertation Technion)

Foresight in terms of market choice can lead to foresight in terms of choosing 'who you are and will be as a company'. This is a subtle activity – yet one that is of great significance! An identity, once more widely known, cannot be changed easily. Hence, it is important to consider your range of market opportunities when developing and shaping your ideas of what your firm is and will be about.

Augury's founders, for example, define themselves as 'a firm that brings predictive maintenance to new markets by listening to machines'. In fact, their tag line says: 'Machines talk. We listen'. This definition of 'who we are' is broad enough and holds for any type of machine or market.

Shaping the culture

A firm's culture is based on the notion of identity, yet it emphasises the shared assumptions, values and beliefs that shape how people behave in a firm. Every organisation develops and maintains a unique culture. Whether a firm's culture is actively shaped or not, it will emerge nonetheless . . . but maybe not in the way that is most beneficial to the success of the firm. Your Agile Focus Strategy will influence the culture that you want to develop and see flourish in your venture. In particular, you can work on implementing a culture that values agility and innovativeness, as these features are instrumental not only in pursuing an Agile Focus Strategy but also for becoming and remaining competitive.

Augury's founders, for example, initiate breakout sessions in which their employees gather together and brainstorm for new ideas. These gatherings nurture the innovative culture of the firm.

Designing the structure of your organisation

Lastly, your foresight of market opportunities is likely to shape the structure of your organisation. You may define the roles in the organisation, or may want to build your divisions in a way that will be aligned with your current and future market entry plans. Remember that these plans may change over time, so the most important element is to structure your firm such that it remains agile!

Your branding and marketing communications

The information shown on the Dartboard is also a key input to your branding strategy and your marketing communications. Now that you have mapped out your future growth path, you have opened up the opportunity to pick a brand name that reflects best what your company is and will be about!

For instance, if you choose a brand name that is focused on one particular application of your abilities, you may lose the ability to sell future products for new markets with the same brand name (e.g., think of the brand names 'Salesforce.com' vs. 'Oracle'). While there are benefits to having a focused brand name that corresponds to a particular application – especially if your budget for marketing communication is limited – you also need to consider its inflexibility when seeking to enter new markets.

Furthermore, changing a brand name down the road means losing the reputation and the positioning that you worked so hard to achieve, and usually requires some significant financial investment.

GetTaxi is one interesting example of such a case. GetTaxi developed a GPS-based application that connects customers and taxi drivers. Yet, over time it became clear that the very same application can also be used for getting anything on demand (from beauty and home services to dry cleaning and food). This novel understanding of what the firm's market opportunities can be required changing the brand name to 'Gett', a move that involved significant expenditures.

So, when you develop and design your brand name and marketing communication strategy, make sure they do not lock you out of possible growth or pivoting options.

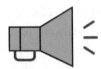

Your fundraising campaign: communicating with potential investors

Investors are often critical to the success of commercialisation efforts. Before they invest, however, they want to understand how much value can be generated with your venture project and want to see the roadmap that will help you to achieve your value creation goals.

The Market Opportunity Navigator allows you to showcase the potential inherent in your venture in a simple and intuitive way, as you can communicate your market opportunities and your market entry strategy to investors, discuss risk mitigation strategies (i.e., Backup Options) and show how you align your funding needs with key milestones and your market roll-out plan.

In order to benefit from the systematic approach and clear language that the Market Opportunity Navigator offers, you can include the main outcomes of your Navigator process in your pitch deck and business plan. For example, investors will appreciate if you can clearly show why you chose your target market opportunity, and how you estimate its value creation potential and its value capture challenge. They will want to see that you are focusing on the most promising opportunity, but also that you understand how to bring your company to the next stage by exploiting additional Growth Options over time.

Moreover, investors understand that innovative projects are often fraught with high levels of uncertainty – hence, when you are able to show your Backup Options, you will signal that you are in command of your venturing process and are ready to navigate into an uncertain future.

Remember that investors are looking for a winning team and not just for a winning idea. Applying the Navigator also signals to investors that your team is rigorous and prudent, with broad insights and long-term views.

3.2 Ongoing use of the Navigator

Are you running in the right direction?

This question bothers entrepreneurs and innovators not only as they choose their initial path but also over time as they strive to pursue it.

Doubts that poke your confidence arise for many reasons. They can result from external changes in your business environment or internal modifications in your firm's abilities. Whatever it may be, you can always go back to the structured evaluation offered by the Navigator, check your new assumptions, support or refute your doubts and align your strategy if necessary. It will build up your confidence – if your analysis shows that you are still running in the right direction, or it will help you to discover a new direction – if your analysis indicates that pivoting is preferable.

New opportunities that come unannounced often create big doubts as well. Think of potential customers that hear about your technology or product and knock on your door to see if it could be used in their domain. Surely, interested customers are great. But should you really span your limited attention or redirect your strategy because of that? The Market Opportunity Navigator can help you in dealing with such decisions: evaluate these new opportunities, look at them relative to your other options and arrive at an informed decision on whether they are worthwhile to be pursued – now or later.

Running in the right direction is also a relevant question when it's time to grow your business. Whether you are still a start-up or a larger enterprise, the Navigator will come handy as you search for your next pathway to success.

All in all, the Market Opportunity Navigator can be of great value throughout your entrepreneurial journey. Applying this framework over time will not only help you in setting a promising strategy but will also help you in developing a proper DNA for your emerging venture – one that facilitates a structured and thorough process when important decisions are on the table.

> *The Market Opportunity Navigator is your ongoing companion. Make it a habit to use it!*

How can you benefit from the Market Opportunity Navigator over time?

Trace back, track and update your decision

☐ Move from intuition, to informed intuition, to fact-based decisions. Use the Navigator with the information that you currently have in hand to decide on your next action items (such as: What shall we work on this week?) until you are sufficiently knowledgeable to set your strategy.

☐ Learn more about your current market opportunities and update their positioning on the Attractiveness Map and, perhaps, on the Agile Focus Dartboard.

☐ Systematically work with newly arising market opportunities, that is, position them on the Attractiveness Map and consider them for an updated Agile Focus Dartboard.

☐ Make your learning process and the evolution of your venture visible to everyone.

☐ Date your updates and save them so that you can always go back for a review. This will help you to understand what has changed and how the logic of your strategy has developed over time.

Navigate the pivoting process

☐ Things may go wrong and you will need to pivot over time. The Agile Focus Strategy helps you to cope with pivoting more easily, as you develop wider capabilities, have Backup Options in store and have been able to learn about other opportunities all along.

☐ Update the Attractiveness Map and the Agile Focus Strategy to make your pivoting choice more apparent.

Navigate the growth process

☐ The Agile Focus Strategy helps you to see and exploit new Growth Options. Once your efforts prove successful, you can use the Market Opportunity Navigator to decide on your new target opportunities. Attractiveness and relatedness will most probably be your main considerations, as emphasised in Worksheet 3.

☐ Remember that you may also use the options that you have placed in storage as licensing opportunities, thereby creating an important additional income stream.

3.3 Using the Market Opportunity Navigator with other business tools

Designing your business strategy is a complicated task that involves an iterative process of learning, planning and validating. A handful of great business tools and methods can help you as you strive to overcome this challenge and set a winning strategy.

This is why we designed the Market Opportunity Navigator in a way that . . .

☐ Allows seamless integration with other major business tools

☐ Mutually reinforces other tools, making their use more valuable

In the following, we explain how the Market Opportunity Navigator can be used together with the Business Model Canvas and the Value Proposition Canvas, outstanding frameworks for planning your strategy, and with the Lean Start-up Methodology – a key method for validating your strategy. Together, they form a powerful suite of tools that clearly lays out the planning and validating processes, as you strive to find your promising path.

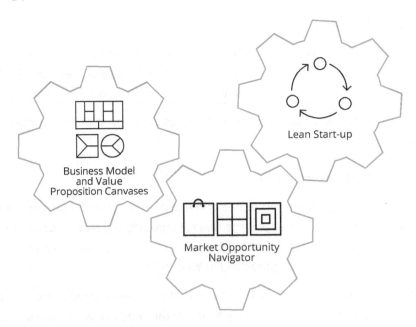

Business Model
and Value
Proposition Canvases

Lean Start-up

Market Opportunity
Navigator

The Business Model and Value Proposition Canvases – Enhancing your frameworks for strategic planning

While the Market Opportunity Navigator provides an excellent framework for assessing your complete landscape of opportunities, the Business Model and Value Proposition Canvases provide great frameworks for zooming into the details of a specific market opportunity.

The Business Model Canvas, developed by Alexander Osterwalder and Yves Pigneur, is one of the most commonly used tools for designing a business model.

It captures the offering (value proposition), the customers (customer segments, distribution channels, relationships), the infrastructure (resources, activities, partners) and the finances (costs, revenues) in a single, easy-to-use template that seeks to explain how a business wants to create value with its offerings.

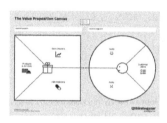

The Value Proposition Canvas, developed by Alexander Osterwalder, Yves Pigneur, Greg Bernarda and Alan Smith, zooms in on two key cells of the Business Model Canvas, that is, the value proposition and the customer segment. This canvas helps innovators to find the fit between their offering (on its left side) and their customers (on its right side). In particular, by analysing and designing the different elements of this canvas, innovators can better understand how to build an attractive offering that will create value for their customers.°

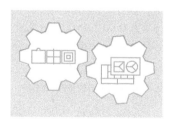

The Market Opportunity Navigator integrates seamlessly with the Business Model and Value Proposition Canvases, and offers great value in addition to these frameworks. These tools work together like cogwheels, with one reinforcing the other, as they provide different levels of analysis that are all essential for setting your strategy.

To find out more take a look at:

° To find out more about the Business Model Canvas and the Value Proposition Canvas, take a look at the creators of the canvases: Strategyzer and strategyzer.com

Combining macro and micro views

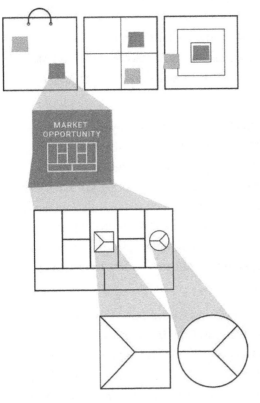

The Navigator provides a powerful 'macro view' on the landscape of opportunities. Each market opportunity in this landscape represents an application of your abilities for a specific set of customers.

As such, it allows you to understand the content of and the links between four core elements of the Business Model Canvas: the 'resources' and the 'activities' that form your unique abilities, the 'value proposition' and the 'customers' cells.

Eventually, each market opportunity should have a clear 'micro planning' that details its business model (i.e., how to create value to the firm) and its value proposition (i.e., how to create value to the customers).

However, to set these elements properly, you need to understand all levels of analysis, as they are all essential: the macro view is essential for uncovering and comparing your options, so that you can choose which markets to play in, and the micro view is essential for understanding how to actually play in that market.

Each level of analysis provides important inputs to the others, so you can drill down and go up in an iterative manner. For instance, you will need to understand your Value Proposition Canvas to be able to evaluate a market opportunity and map it on the Attractiveness Map, and you will need to understand your Agile Focus Strategy, to be able to design a winning business model.

Design your business model to address an attractive market opportunity

The birds-eye view of the Navigator will help you to choose the most attractive market opportunity, so that you can design a winning business model to address this promising path.

Most importantly, it answers the question 'Which customer segment(s) is (are) the best to address with your resources? This is often one of the most pressing questions that an innovator has, and without having a good answer to it, the business model design process will suffer.

Design your business model to be flexible

You can design the building blocks of your business model in a flexible manner, to align with your Agile Focus Strategy. Think about your partners, your channels, your key activities and resources or even the type of relationships that you build with your customers. They can all be designed with your smart portfolio in mind, to enable a smoother pivoting or an easier growth in the future.

In order to get inspiration for your business model design, you can also turn to the Business Model Navigator, which offers a collection of 55 models that have been implemented successfully![o]

In sum, the combination of the Market Opportunity Navigator with the Business Model and Value Proposition Canvases offers powerful insights that reach significantly beyond the insights that each tool can provide by itself. These tools reinforce each other to provide the comprehensive planning that is required for finding the most fertile ground for your endeavour.

In fact, it doesn't matter which of these cogwheels you start rolling first. Eventually, you will need all to formulate a winning strategy.

o To find out more take a look at: The Business Model Navigator/ Gassmann, Frankenberger & Csik (2014)

The Lean Start-up Methodology –
Enhancing your processes for strategic validation

The Lean Start-up Methodology, which was developed by Eric Ries and Steve Blank, has risen to prominence as it offers innovators a process by which they can rapidly test, learn and adapt their offerings for their customers. It adds great value to the Market Opportunity Navigator, as it forces you to nail down and validate your assumptions as you learn about your market opportunities.

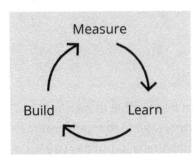

In particular, this methodology proposes that innovators have to discover and validate their target customers before they engage in product development and company building. Hence, innovators should adopt rapid build – measure – learn cycles that involve the formulation of assumptions, their validation or their adaptation – if required.°

The Market Opportunity Navigator and the Lean Start-up Methodology complement each other in several ways. Just as before, the two approaches work together like cogwheels, with one reinforcing the other.

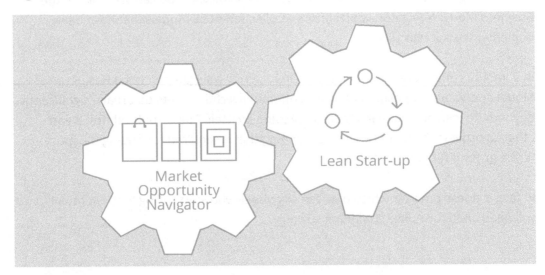

° To find out more take a look at: The Lean Startup/ Eric Ries (2011); The Four Steps to the Epiphany/ Steve Blank (2005); Running Lean/ Ash Maurya (2010); Lean strategy/ David Collis (2016)

Here is how you can greatly benefit from using these tools together:

1. Combine planning and experimentation

The Navigator is a tool to plan your strategy, reflect on what you have learned and adjust if necessary. This plan-reflect-adjust process enhances the rapid experimentation cycles offered by the Lean Methodology. Together they create a complete learning process, during which you can be both predictive and adaptive. The iterative process usually begins with planning. Gather the knowledge that you have in hand on the Navigator to understand and to set your strategic boundaries so that you can engage in meaningful experimentations. Then build a minimum viable product and get out of the building – as guided by the Lean Method – to learn about real customer needs. You can then go back to the Navigator to reflect and adjust: update your Market Opportunity Set, your Attractiveness Map, and your Agile Focus Dartboard according to what you have learned. Now build-measure-learn again . . .

In short, the Navigator offers a process to rigorously plan and define your market domains and the Lean Method offers a process to understand and to validate the customers' needs, as these are often not known in advance, even with rigorous planning.

2. Combine broad and targeted perspectives

The Lean Method pushes you to examine a single, targeted path. If it turns out to be the 'wrong' one, you should pivot by finding a branch from that path that seems to be interesting. The Market Opportunity Navigator, however, guides you to see the broad landscape of opportunities. This overview can save you from going down the wrong path in your experimentation or from missing out a more promising one. In addition, it enables you to be more prepared for pivoting down the road, as you keep on reflecting on your Market Opportunity Set, and you keep some options open following your Agile Focus Strategy.

In short, this broad perspective helps you to find a 'global maximum' rather than a local one, and to leverage your variety of options for a better manoeuvrability.

3. Combine customers and market hypotheses

The Lean Method pushes you to validate your hypotheses about customers through rapid experimentations. These hypotheses are usually based on the nine building blocks of the Business Model Canvas and emphasise mainly the value proposition aspect. The Navigator examines the attractiveness of an opportunity based on its Potential and its Challenge. The structured evaluation shown in Worksheet 2 forms the basis for an additional set of hypotheses which examines other aspects of the market and its environmental context (such as competitors, value chain actors etc.) so that you can generate market hypotheses on top of your customer hypotheses and base your strategic choice on a more inclusive set of considerations.

4. Combine short and long learning loops

The Lean Method emphasises the importance of rapid build-measure-learn loops. Yet, as examples such as KalOptics and Microbot have shown, many ideas simply cannot be tested quickly and cheaply in a series of experiments. They require significant upfront investment in research and development, perhaps even over a longer term. They may also be too novel or too complex to allow rapid customer assessments. In other words, firms with such innovations need to incur substantial expenses – and thus need to be very careful about the path which they want to take. If this is the case for you, the Market Opportunity Navigator will provide you with important answers, as you can apply it to identify the most promising paths and to make sure that you remain agile if adaptation is required over time. The Agile Focus Strategy is therefore indispensable when rapid experimentation is not feasible.

In sum, the combination of the Navigator and the Lean Start-up Methodology is powerful, as they reinforce each other to create a broad and complete process for validating your strategy. Once again, it doesn't matter which of these cogwheels you start rolling first. Eventually, you will need both to formulate a winning strategy.

4

Beyond start-ups: The Navigator for:

Identifying, evaluating and exploiting new market opportunities are core to the venture creation process, the competitiveness of established firms and, more generally, to value creation.

Other than newly created ventures, the Market Opportunity Navigator can provide novel insights and create value for . . .

☐ Established firms – when seeking to commercialise their innovations and looking for new business opportunities

☐ Investors – when screening new ventures and when guiding their growth strategy over time

☐ Technology Transfer Offices – when working with inventors and drafting patent applications

☐ Educators and accelerators – when seeking to provide knowledge and to accompany the learning of budding entrepreneurs and innovators

And . . . even if you are not part of these groups, the Navigator's process (or parts of it) entails valuable insights that may help you to understand your specific business situation in a more thorough way and allow you to arrive at a better strategic choice.

4.1 The Market Opportunity Navigator for established firms

All companies have to renew themselves to survive and are challenged to capture new growth opportunities: they struggle to sustain their competitiveness, find new fertile grounds and satisfy their shareholders.

Yet, discovering and implementing growth endeavours is extremely challenging for established firms. In fact, studies show that a very high percentage of these attempts fail, and that profitable growth is becoming increasingly difficult and more elusive for most companies.[o]

Why is this the case? Organisations are typically designed to protect the status quo and to do well what they are already doing. Hence, they are usually good at execution, but they are rarely designed to engage in the art of entrepreneurship. Finding the right growth opportunity and successfully capturing it requires a change in mindset for most managers and employees. It also requires the cooperation of many different groups of stakeholders – each following their own agenda and incentives, and each possessing different risk preferences that may limit what they are willing to accept as expansion attempts. Overall, as your firm becomes larger, more complex and more internally focused over time, growth is often stifled by the very forces that make your organisation run smoothly and execute in its established lines of business.

In his books 'Profit from the Core' and 'Beyond the Core', Chris Zook emphasises the importance of leveraging existing core abilities of the firm when searching for profitable growth opportunities. These adjacent diversification moves make use of existing customer relationships, technologies or core business skills to build competitive advantage in a new area.[oo]

In fact, when 3M engaged in a study to better understand their own successes and failures, they actually discovered that new businesses based on long-standing 3M competencies were dramatically more likely to succeed than those that didn't leverage core skills.

To find out more take a look at:
o   The Growth Gamble/ Campbell & Park (2005)
oo Beyond the Core/ Chris Zook (2004); Profit from the Core/ Chris Zook (2001)

In addition, successful growth endeavours depend greatly on applying methods that allow you to decide correctly, to tilt the odds in your favour and to control the cost of failures when they inevitably occur. According to Chris Zook, even small improvements in performance along these dimensions can considerably increase the overall likelihood of successfully capturing a new business opportunity.

The Market Opportunity Navigator supports you in accomplishing just that: it will help you to discover new market opportunities stemming from your unique abilities, will guide you towards the most promising opportunities and will help you to control your risks along the way.

So, whether you are the CEO, the VP for business development, the innovation manager of your firm or if you carry any other role that faces the challenge of finding new growth paths, the Market Opportunity Navigator offers several key benefits that will help you in better positioning your intrapreneurial endeavours for success!

Casting a wide net

Before you focus on a specific growth opportunity, you must make sure to develop a broad range of business concepts. Outstanding opportunities are rare, and your chances of stumbling across one such idea are directly proportionate to the number of business opportunities that your company can identify.

Generating a set of new business options requires an explicit process for developing the capability to uncover truly fresh opportunities. Step 1 of the Market Opportunity Navigator offers such an explicit process: it guides you on how to de-link your core abilities from any specific product that you are currently producing or any specific customer that you are currently addressing. It helps you in characterising your core abilities in 'their own right', so that you can search systematically for new market opportunities. Importantly, this process will not only support you in discovering adjacent market opportunities but will also facilitate your distant search for new opportunities – to help you overcome the well-known 'tyranny' of your currently served markets.

Deciding on 'how to decide'

Business expansions are journeys into the unknown. Screening and evaluating your opportunities are therefore both extremely challenging and extremely crucial tasks. In fact, successful companies invest a great deal in developing criteria and processes for making the best growth decisions. For example, such an innovation funnel is used at an innovation centre of Microsoft: their structured, multi-stage process includes four gateways where new opportunities are screened – moving from initial perceptions about many opportunities, to the evaluation of several opportunities, and to developing strategy and tactics for a few opportunities.

The Market Opportunity Navigator offers you a proven and easy-to-apply process for screening, evaluating and mapping your growth opportunities. Step 2 provides you with a comprehensive checklist of criteria for evaluating the Potential and the Challenge inherent in your opportunities, and guides you on how to map their attractiveness in one clear overview. These criteria hold regardless of whether your Growth Options are based on internal means or on external ones such as partnerships and acquisitions.

Depending on your specific needs, you can also adjust the process. For instance, if necessary you can include additional factors that may shape the Potential of an opportunity (e.g., the extent to which it influences existing businesses) or that may shape the Challenge of an opportunity (e.g., the extent to which it fits the organisational culture).

Overall, this thorough evaluation process will help you to remove the weeds and uncover the gems – and make a smart growth decision.

Bringing relatedness to the forefront

Assessing relatedness among opportunities has two main implications:

First, you can use the relatedness measure to understand the linkage between your current business and a new Growth Option. Chris Zook suggests that relatedness to a strong core is the most powerful engine for value creation and shows that many of the most successful growth companies were able to maintain strong reinforcement between the current business and the new adjacencies. Therefore, assessing the relative distance of alternative growth opportunities to your current business is useful when comparing possible investments relative to each other, as well as in evaluating them on an absolute basis.

Second, once a growth opportunity is anchored as your preferred option, you can use relatedness to adopt a long-term perspective and plan your multi-step moves. In other words, you can build a portfolio of related Growth and Backup Options around this primary opportunity. Furthermore, relatedness reasoning can also help you in building 'clusters of future moves' around each possible investment option and in comparing these different strategic scenarios by having the bigger picture of all opportunities in mind.

Afterall, investment in one opportunity always carries the trade-off of putting aside other possibilities, so understanding future portfolios is important for making the right choice.

Worksheet 3 offers clear guidance on how to assess product and market relatedness. You can use these measures for both purposes: to assess the relatedness of an opportunity to your current business and to build a portfolio of options around it. This will help you in setting the right priorities, in spending cash with the right amount of foresight and, ultimately, in reaping the greatest benefits from your innovation efforts!

Controlling the risk

One of the biggest challenges in innovation and growth projects is managing the risk inherent in such endeavours. As a manager, you have to make sure to maintain the net income from your established lines of business while also managing riskier growth projects: you need to exploit the existing business and explore new businesses. The Market Opportunity Navigator can help you in balancing the risky growth projects and in controlling the cost of failure once it occurs. In particular, the Agile Focus Strategy provides foresight on your opportunities for backup and future expansion, and leads to a smart portfolio of options that you keep open. This is an excellent way to hedge your bets and to prepare your firm for potential pivots. Having such foresight will signal to your different stakeholders that you are taking an informed risk rather than an unreasonable gamble.

Selling the idea within the organisation

Lastly, one major challenge is to get the agreement, the support and the commitment of all stakeholders on a future growth path. In the early stages of a new project, you will need at least a sponsor and a small incubation team to embark on the idea. The Market Opportunity Navigator can help you in several ways as you strive to promote your idea within the firm.

First, it helps to establish a common language within the organisation to facilitate discussions and reach agreements. The stages of the decision process are clearly specified and visualised – so that you can discuss opportunities in a more efficient and effective manner, either with your peers or in prominent board meetings.

Second, forming a clear strategic vision, as the Navigator suggests, is key when trying to lead change and create commitment in your firm. According to John Kotter, author of 'Leading Change', communicating a clear plan and keeping it updated and breathing are necessary when trying to sell your idea in the organisation.[o]

Lastly, Kotter also suggests that generating short-term wins can greatly help in getting the agreement and the sponsorship for your main idea. Hence, you can use the Attractiveness Map to identify your 'Quick Wins' and to design your strategy accordingly.

All in all, the Market Opportunity Navigator can serve as an invaluable tool that allows you not only to identify and exploit major new opportunities for growth but also to build a systematic capability in this core activity: the *capability of opportunity management*.[oo] This capability includes superior skills in identifying a larger number, and a more varied set of new opportunities, in evaluating and prioritising these alternatives in an efficient manner and in assembling a promising opportunity portfolio.

With the Market Opportunity Navigator, you can find out how to best leverage the current assets of the firm to find the next BIG thing and how to manage your innovation funnel more effectively.

As a side note, it is interesting to mention that the Navigator's process is useful not only for comparing different market opportunities and setting the growth strategy of a firm but also for setting priorities among different investment options within a department or a specific unit. For instance, a product manager that needs to decide which features to develop in the upcoming year can use the very same process to set his priorities properly. Of course, the factors that shape the Potential and the Challenge of his options will likely have to be adjusted, but the overall framework will still be of help. In sum, the Navigator can actually be applied in different levels of the organisation, by different types of managers, for different types of investment choices.

---

o   To find out more take a look at: Leading Change/ John Kotter (1996)
oo To find out more about opportunity management in established firms take a look at: The Entrepreneurial Mindset/ McGrath & MacMillan (2000); Discovery-Driven Growth/ McGrath & MacMillan (2009); The End of Competitive Advantage/ Rita McGrath (2013); The process of technological competence leveraging/ Erwin Danneels (2007)

4.2 The Market Opportunity Navigator for investors

The Market Opportunity Navigator can support investors in two main ways. First, it allows for a more effective screening of new ventures and the opportunities that they seek to exploit. Second, it allows for an improved management of their portfolio companies over time.

Whether you are a private investor, a corporate investor or a venture capitalist, you can enjoy the benefits of the Navigator in several ways.

Supporting the screening process in investment decisions

As an investor, you primarily look for venture deals that allow for significant growth and in a relatively short period (often within a time frame of 5–7 years max). One of the main reasons as to why you turn off a funding request is because you believe that the venture's target market does not offer the potential for significant value creation, or at least not within this time frame . . . in some cases, however, founders fail to communicate the potential inherent in their venture, although it does exist!

The Market Opportunity Navigator offers a highly compelling way with which ventures can communicate their opportunities and associated market entry strategy to potential investors. In particular, it allows entrepreneurs to showcase the potential inherent in their venture, discuss risk mitigation strategies (i.e., Backup Options) and align their funding needs with the key milestones and future growth. It also helps them to bridge the knowledge gaps and the different perspectives that each side brings to the table.

In turn, you are better able to grasp the strategic plans of founders and understand the prospects of a venture proposal. You can also communicate your feedback to founders in a more effective manner – for instance, if you believe the venture has merits yet fails to exploit the best market opportunity.

Furthermore, you can get additional insights on other key elements shaping your investment decision when founding teams apply the Navigator, as you can understand how they manage their opportunities and how flexible their thinking is.

> *Investors can request founders to use the Navigator in their pitch deck – thus allowing a thorough discussion on alternative market opportunities and on a validated roadmap.*

Overall, the Market Opportunity Navigator enhances your ability to communicate with founders, and to make better and quicker investment choices.

Supporting the management of portfolio companies

Once an investment is made, you and the founders have a vital interest in seeing the venture flourish. During the venture development process, the Market Opportunity Navigator can serve as an important tool that supports venture management – for instance, in terms of planning and executing pivots to alternative markets or for pursuing additional growth opportunities.

The navigator also offers a clear language that facilitates fruitful discussions in board meetings and aligns expectations of different stakeholders, once a strategy needs to be set.

4.3 The Market Opportunity Navigator for Technology Transfer Offices

One of the core missions of Technology Transfer Offices (TTOs) is to transfer knowledge and technologies from universities and other research institutions to a wide range of users, to ensure that such advances can be exploited widely in the form of new products, services, processes etc. The process of technology commercialisation involves mechanisms such as new venture creation, licensing agreements, partnerships and joint ventures. The basis of many such agreements is the patent, as it codifies the technological knowledge that is to be commercialised.

Technology Transfer Offices typically have strong legal expertise, as such expertise is needed for both the patenting process as well as the contractual arrangements made between the parties. They also draw on strong technological expertise – expertise that is either present in their own team or that the inventor provides to the TTO.

Yet, among the many TTOs that we observed, knowledge about market opportunities and associated applications remained limited – in no small part because such knowledge requires a different set of skills and competences, that are often scarce among the relatively small TTO teams.

So, if you are a team member of a technology transfer unit, you can use the Market Opportunity Navigator to improve your work. In essence, applying the Navigator on a research project – either by you or by the inventor him- or herself – will provide you with an improved view of the potential applications for the technology. Such an improved view will support you in a number of ways, including:

- Getting a better understanding of the value of a proposed technology, to decide which technologies are worthwhile to be pursued, and which are not

- Making better commercialisation decisions (which opportunities should be exploited with which mechanism)

- Writing stronger patents as the application space is more clearly specified

- Having better knowledge of potential licensees and other partners

- Drafting more specific agreements with partners

In addition, the Market Opportunity Navigator can serve as an excellent communication tool between you and the inventor. It allows you to better understand the technology – in its own right – and realise its limits and possibilities, and it allows the researcher to better understand the applicability of his work and the additional know-how that may still be required to capture its value at the fullest.

Notably, TTOs can commercialise a technology in several ways simultaneously. You can license a technology to different parties in parallel, based on exclusivity in different domains, or you can support the creation of several spin-outs based on the same patent. Thus, the Agile Focus Strategy – which is elemental for resource-constrained ventures – has limited relevance in the pursuit of multiple commercialisation paths. However, once a technology is commercialised through a spin-out, the Agile Focus Strategy becomes powerful, and the Market Opportunity Navigator can, again, serve as an important tool that supports the management of the venture.

4.4 The Market Opportunity Navigator for educators and accelerators

The Market Opportunity Navigator is a key tool for educators – as it addresses one of the most pressing concerns of start-ups and established firms, that is, how to identify and benefit from opportunities for value creation.

Academic institutes, as well as accelerators, seek to educate their trainees and provide them with valuable knowledge and a toolbox to promote their future success. The Market Opportunity Navigator is an essential part of such a toolbox.

Using the Market Opportunity Navigator in Higher Education

As an educator, you can use the Market Opportunity Navigator in your classroom teaching. With this solid tool at hand, you can teach your students not only how to discover and strategise valuable opportunities but also how to engage in systematic analysis and how they can maintain their cognitive flexibility during the innovation or venture creation process. In short, it is not merely a capability that you can offer to your students but a dynamic capability!

Because the Market Opportunity Navigator is solidly anchored in contemporary thinking in entrepreneurship, innovation and strategy domains, it can readily be integrated into your teaching curricula – either as part of an existing course, a standalone course or in a workshop setting.

In our own teaching efforts, we have achieved extraordinary results using the Navigator process in a wide variety of educational settings. More specifically, we have found that the Navigator process fits well to entrepreneurship, innovation and strategy classes and can be taught to students on the bachelor, master or executive education levels.

Because the Navigator offers a staged framework, it is fairly easy to structure the lectures and the students' assignments, either in class or at home.

The worksheets offer hands-on exercises and fit well the current trend of engaging the students with real, problem-based work. These hands-on assignments can also be presented in class, to facilitate discussions and peer learning.

Furthermore, given that the book and its supporting material explain both the theoretical background and its practical implementations in an easy-to-use format, they offer an excellent teaching companion for you and an important learning companion for your students.

Some insights can help you as you design your course:

First, we typically include real technologies in our curricula. These can be based on the students' own start-up ideas or on other research projects in the university. Working on these 'real' cases not only motivates students but also helps the innovators . . . and, ultimately, may create significant value!

Second, we have found that a mix of students pursuing a business education and of students having no prior education in business (e.g., students in a variety of engineering domains) works best for such classes, as they can contribute different perspectives and expertise to the three steps of the Market Opportunity Navigator. So, if feasible, try to gather a varied audience in your class.

To give you a rough idea on how you can apply the Navigator, an example for a workshop structure on market opportunities for new technologies is shown below.

Suggested workshop:
Market opportunities for new technologies

Preparation: Scouting for technologies (either by lecturer or by enrolled students)

WEEK I   Background, explanation of the Market Opportunity Navigator
and its Worksheets 1, 2 and 3

WEEK II   Presentation of technologies (by inventors)
Team-building: teams of 3–4 students work on one technology
Joint (class-wide) brainstorming of market opportunities
Worksheet 1: preliminary draft
Start filling the Market Opportunity Set per technology
Homework: continue opportunity identification and use Worksheet 2
for evaluation

Time for students to work on opportunity identification and evaluation

WEEK III   Presentations of the results (Market Opportunity Set and
Attractiveness Map) and backup Worksheets 1 and 2

WEEK IV   Workshop with externals (e.g., VCs, Angels, start-up consultants) to
advance understanding of market opportunities and their evaluations
Homework: improve existing insights and use Worksheet 3

Time for students to work on developing the Agile Focus Strategy

WEEK V   Final Presentations:
Market Opportunity Set, Attractiveness Map and Agile Focus Dartboard
Invite inventors and other stakeholders for their
feedback and learning

Using the Navigator in accelerators and incubators

Accelerators and incubators are constantly searching for ways to boost their start-ups' success. In fact, acceleration programmes are primarily developed to nurture earlystage founders and to provide them with the necessary platforms and know-hows for value creation. Moreover, the success of accelerators and incubators themselves depends largely on the success of their start-ups!

Whether you run an accelerator programme or train its start-ups, the Market Opportunity Navigator is an ideal add-on to your programme. Similar to other business tools (e.g., the Business Model Canvas), the Navigator can be easily taught and applied throughout the incubation period. You can schedule a joint workshop or one-on-one meetings to help founders in identifying, evaluating and setting their market opportunity strategy smartly. This training is visual and fun. You can put the Navigator's main boards on the wall, and use sticky notes to show the market opportunities that were identified and considered by each group. Presenting the three steps of the Navigator can facilitate interesting discussions and generate excellent peer learning – which is of vital importance for early stage founders.

Because many start-ups already have a market opportunity in mind as they enter the programme, they can start with Step 2 of the Navigator to evaluate how valuable their opportunity is and to map it on the Attractiveness Map. Once this analysis is accomplished, founders can see whether it is worthwhile to pursue this opportunity as their primary market. Regardless of their decision, however, it is then important to go back to Step 1, generate additional market opportunities, evaluate them, and design the Agile Focus Strategy of the firm accordingly. In the process, they may discover even better opportunities . . .

Furthermore, as the Navigator is most beneficial if it is used in an ongoing manner, it can actually serve as a reflection tool during the acceleration period and, thus, accompany the learning process. Founders can update their Navigator in a timely manner, to summarise what they have learned so far, and discuss their strategy-building progress in a shared language.

Overall, the Market Opportunity Navigator is an extremely important tool for early stage ventures and can greatly contribute to their success – and to the success of your accelerator or incubator!

5

Epilogue:
The Navigator's Navigator

Setting the strategy for the Market Opportunity Navigator

The Market Opportunity Navigator is a business tool that supports entrepreneurs in setting their market opportunity strategy.

As we began developing it, however, it became clear that our unique know-how – on which this tool is built – can actually be utilised to serve other needs of other market segments. We had to identify and examine these options and prioritise them, if we wanted to develop an appealing offering to an attractive market. In other words, we had to follow our own advice and use the tool ourselves. Here is how we used the Market Opportunity Navigator – for the Navigator . . .

The first step was to analyse our unique abilities and search broadly to uncover additional market opportunities, thus creating our Market Opportunity Set. Worksheet 1 came in handy for that purpose:

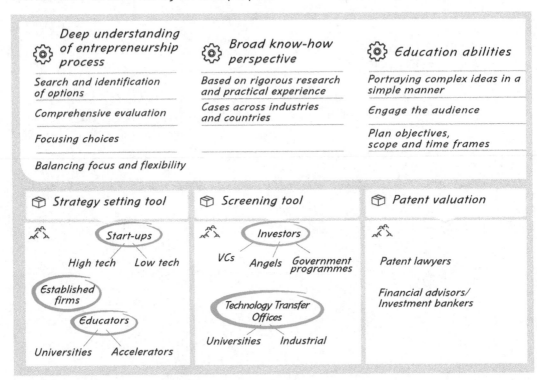

First and foremost, our unique know-how is built on the deep understanding that we possess regarding the entrepreneurial process, including the identification of options, their evaluation criteria, the choice mechanism and the challenge of balancing focus and flexibility when making this profound decision. This know-how is also based on a broad perspective, as it relies on extensive academic research and practical experience, and is grounded by hundreds of cases across industries and countries. We also have unique abilities as educators – as we are both well-recognised lecturers in the field, with all that it entails.

These unique abilities can be applied to create a strategy-setting tool for managing the choice of market opportunities that can be used by start-ups, established firms and educators of all kind. They can also be applied as a screening tool – especially for investors and Technology Transfer Offices, where difficult screening decisions are core to their business' success. Additionally, we could apply our abilities to create a method for patent valuations, which can be useful for patent lawyers or financial advisors such as investment bankers, to list a few.

As we began to investigate these options and to talk with different potential customers, we understood that the patent valuation application was currently too far out of our expertise and thus decided to assess the following five markets: start-ups, educators, established firms, investors and Technology Transfer Offices. Our Market Opportunity Set was ready for the next stage:

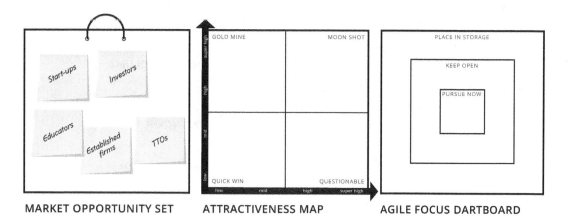

MARKET OPPORTUNITY SET   ATTRACTIVENESS MAP   AGILE FOCUS DARTBOARD

We next used Worksheet 2 to evaluate each of these markets.

Start-ups:

New ventures, of all kind, are the original users that we had in mind when we started this project. We evaluated the overall Potential of this market opportunity as 'high' and the overall Challenge of pursuing it as 'mid'. Here are the major considerations that lead us to this evaluation:

We understand the needs of start-ups very well and can comfortably score their compelling reason to buy as high. Time and time again we saw entrepreneurs struggling with their market choice, with no structured framework to support them well enough

The market volume is super high: according to research by the Global Entrepreneurship Monitor, over 15 million adults (18–64 year old) are actively engaged in launching a new firm in the USA, in the UK the number is around 2 million and globally 388 million

The economic viability of this market is 'mid', as start-ups are simply not well-funded entities. Although we designed the Navigator as an ongoing companion which increases customers' stickiness, the overall margins in selling a book or a software are not high

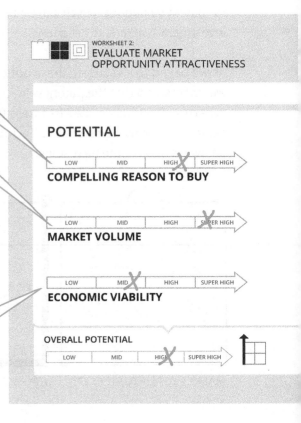

WORKSHEET 2:
EVALUATE MARKET
OPPORTUNITY ATTRACTIVENESS

POTENTIAL

| LOW | MID | HIGH | SUPER HIGH |

COMPELLING REASON TO BUY

| LOW | MID | HIGH | SUPER HIGH |

MARKET VOLUME

| LOW | MID | HIGH | SUPER HIGH |

ECONOMIC VIABILITY

OVERALL POTENTIAL

| LOW | MID | HIGH | SUPER HIGH |

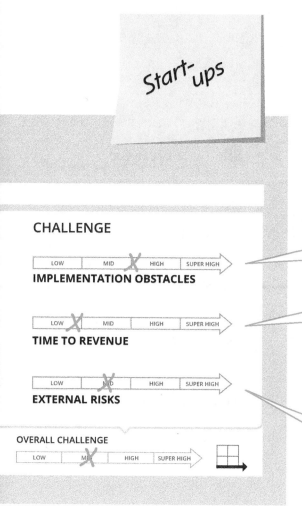

CHALLENGE

LOW	MID	HIGH	SUPER HIGH

IMPLEMENTATION OBSTACLES

We assessed that the implementation obstacles would be 'mid-high': although we knew quite well what our product should include, we would still need to invest quite a lot in developing a friendly and easy-to-use interface, and in accessing this market

LOW	MID	HIGH	SUPER HIGH

TIME TO REVENUE

We estimated that the time to revenue would be relatively short, because the market is ready and sales cycles are short

LOW	MID	HIGH	SUPER HIGH

EXTERNAL RISKS

The external risks that we will be confronting are estimated as 'mid', especially because there are many books out there providing good advice for entrepreneurs

OVERALL CHALLENGE

LOW	MID	HIGH	SUPER HIGH

Educators:

Being educators ourselves – teaching technology commercialisation and entrepreneurship courses in universities – we are highly familiar with this market and can access it relatively easily.

We estimated the overall Potential of this market to be 'high' and the overall Challenge as 'mid'. Here are the major considerations that lead us to this evaluation:

As educators, we are highly familiar with the un-met need that this market confronts: the need for powerful, easy-to-teach frameworks that can be applied in class to help trainees become better entrepreneurs

The market volume is significant and growing: universities across the globe flag their entrepreneurship programmes, on-line courses are booming and the number of accelerators has grown from just a handful a few years ago to more than 600 globally today

The economic viability of this market is high, especially because universities and accelerators are able to pay for high quality workshops and seminars, where our margins could be sufficient

WORKSHEET 2:
EVALUATE MARKET OPPORTUNITY ATTRACTIVENESS

POTENTIAL

| LOW | MID | HIGH | SUPER HIGH |
COMPELLING REASON TO BUY

| LOW | MID | HIGH | SUPER HIGH |
MARKET VOLUME

| LOW | MID | HIGH | SUPER HIGH |
ECONOMIC VIABILITY

OVERALL POTENTIAL
| LOW | MID | HIGH | SUPER HIGH |

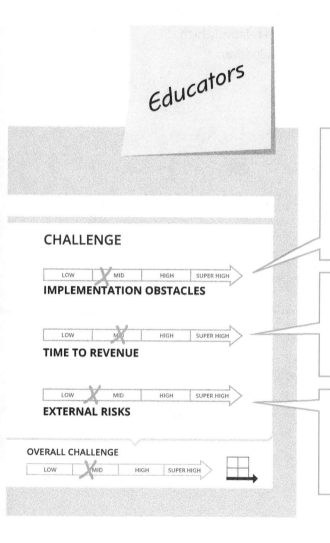

CHALLENGE

| LOW | X MID | HIGH | SUPER HIGH |

IMPLEMENTATION OBSTACLES

| LOW | MID | HIGH | SUPER HIGH |

TIME TO REVENUE

| LOW | X MID | HIGH | SUPER HIGH |

EXTERNAL RISKS

OVERALL CHALLENGE

| LOW | X MID | HIGH | SUPER HIGH |

Once the tool is developed, it would be relatively easy for us to build a course around it and to access the educational market with our current connections and networks

Time to revenue was a bit higher than for start-ups, because sales may take a while – especially when selling workshops to universities and accelerators

External risks are relatively low, because business tools for budding entrepreneurs are not that common, and the market is clearly receptive to innovative ideas

Established firms:

Established firms must innovate to maintain their competitiveness and to identify new growth opportunities . . . or else they are bound to lose market share and eventually die. Managers in established firms can apply the Market Opportunity Navigator to identify and prioritise their Growth Options.

We estimated that the overall Potential of this market is somewhere between high to super high, but that the overall Challenge in pursuing it is relatively high.
Here are the major considerations that lead us to this evaluation:

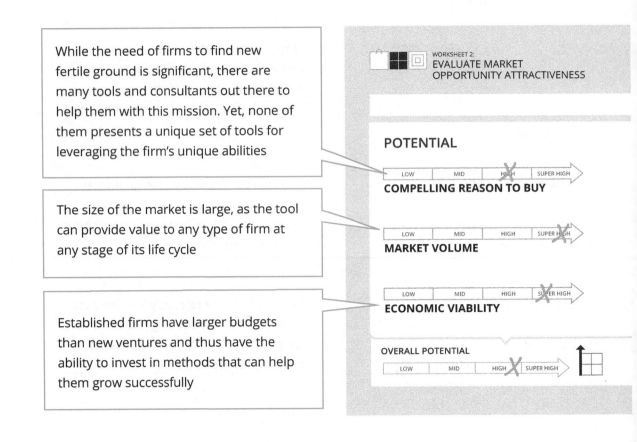

While the need of firms to find new fertile ground is significant, there are many tools and consultants out there to help them with this mission. Yet, none of them presents a unique set of tools for leveraging the firm's unique abilities

The size of the market is large, as the tool can provide value to any type of firm at any stage of its life cycle

Established firms have larger budgets than new ventures and thus have the ability to invest in methods that can help them grow successfully

WORKSHEET 2:
EVALUATE MARKET
OPPORTUNITY ATTRACTIVENESS

POTENTIAL

| LOW | MID | HIGH | SUPER HIGH |

COMPELLING REASON TO BUY

| LOW | MID | HIGH | SUPER HIGH |

MARKET VOLUME

| LOW | MID | HIGH | SUPER HIGH |

ECONOMIC VIABILITY

OVERALL POTENTIAL

| LOW | MID | HIGH | SUPER HIGH |

Established firms

CHALLENGE

| LOW | MID | HIGH | SUPER HIGH |

IMPLEMENTATION OBSTACLES

Accessing this market will be relatively difficult for us, and sales will require unique efforts. Product adaptations might also be required

| LOW | MID | HIGH | SUPER HIGH |

TIME TO REVENUE

Time to revenue is expected to be high because sales cycles and deployment are likely to be long

| LOW | MID | HIGH | SUPER HIGH |

EXTERNAL RISKS

The risks we are facing here are relatively high, because established firms can often be closed-minded and place major emphasis on their current markets

OVERALL CHALLENGE

| LOW | MID | HIGH | SUPER HIGH |

Technology Transfer Offices:

Technology Transfer Offices are dedicated to identifying research which has potential commercial interest and to develop the strategies for how to exploit it. TTOs work on behalf of universities and research institutions, governments and even large corporations. They can use the Market Opportunity Navigator as a screening tool – to fully understand the potential of an innovation and decide whether they should invest efforts in its commercialisation (e.g., patents, licenses).

We estimated that the overall Potential of this market is 'mid' and so is the overall Challenge. Here are the major considerations that lead us to this evaluation:

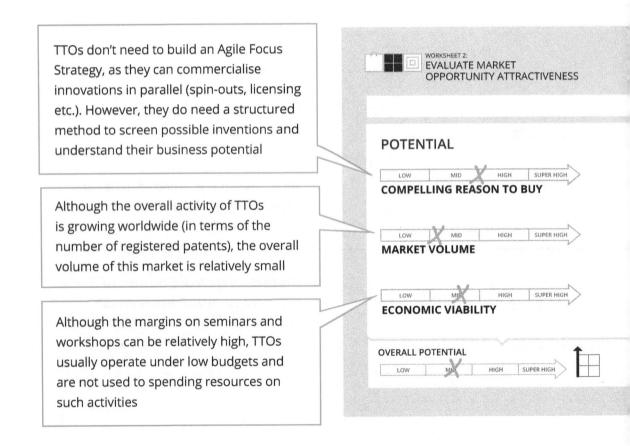

TTOs don't need to build an Agile Focus Strategy, as they can commercialise innovations in parallel (spin-outs, licensing etc.). However, they do need a structured method to screen possible inventions and understand their business potential

Although the overall activity of TTOs is growing worldwide (in terms of the number of registered patents), the overall volume of this market is relatively small

Although the margins on seminars and workshops can be relatively high, TTOs usually operate under low budgets and are not used to spending resources on such activities

WORKSHEET 2:
EVALUATE MARKET OPPORTUNITY ATTRACTIVENESS

POTENTIAL

| LOW | MID | HIGH | SUPER HIGH |

COMPELLING REASON TO BUY

| LOW | MID | HIGH | SUPER HIGH |

MARKET VOLUME

| LOW | MID | HIGH | SUPER HIGH |

ECONOMIC VIABILITY

OVERALL POTENTIAL

| LOW | MID | HIGH | SUPER HIGH |

Technology Transfer Offices

As most of the TTOs belong to universities, we are familiar with these customers and can access them relatively easily, with a product that would be tailored to their specific needs

CHALLENGE

LOW	MID	HIGH	SUPER HIGH

IMPLEMENTATION OBSTACLES

Time to revenue is relatively short, due to short development time and market readiness

LOW	MID	HIGH	SUPER HIGH

TIME TO REVENUE

We estimate the risks as 'mid', mainly because the budget of these customers depends on policies of the university

LOW	MID	HIGH	SUPER HIGH

EXTERNAL RISKS

OVERALL CHALLENGE

LOW	MID	HIGH	SUPER HIGH

Investors:

Investors of early stage start-ups are constantly seeking promising businesses. The Market Opportunity Navigator can assist them in screening their deal-flow, and in achieving agreement with their investment partners.

We estimated that the overall Potential of this market is mid-high and that the overall Challenge of pursuing it is high. Here are the major considerations that lead us to this evaluation:

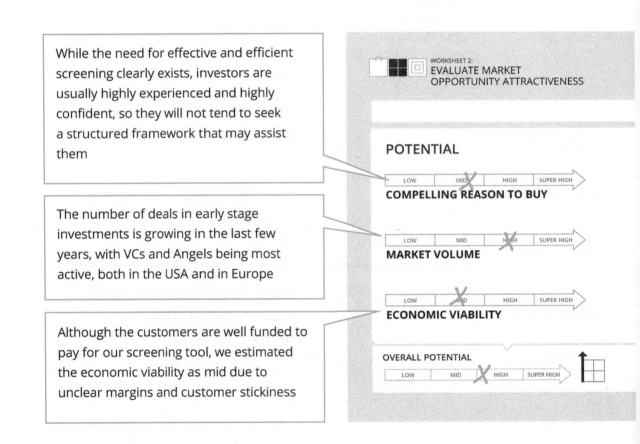

While the need for effective and efficient screening clearly exists, investors are usually highly experienced and highly confident, so they will not tend to seek a structured framework that may assist them

The number of deals in early stage investments is growing in the last few years, with VCs and Angels being most active, both in the USA and in Europe

Although the customers are well funded to pay for our screening tool, we estimated the economic viability as mid due to unclear margins and customer stickiness

WORKSHEET 2:
EVALUATE MARKET
OPPORTUNITY ATTRACTIVENESS

POTENTIAL

LOW | MID | HIGH | SUPER HIGH
COMPELLING REASON TO BUY

LOW | MID | HIGH | SUPER HIGH
MARKET VOLUME

LOW | MID | HIGH | SUPER HIGH
ECONOMIC VIABILITY

OVERALL POTENTIAL
LOW | MID | HIGH | SUPER HIGH

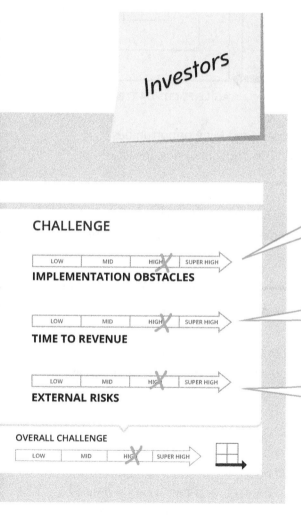

CHALLENGE

| LOW | MID | HIGH | SUPER HIGH |
IMPLEMENTATION OBSTACLES

| LOW | MID | HIGH | SUPER HIGH |
TIME TO REVENUE

| LOW | MID | HIGH | SUPER HIGH |
EXTERNAL RISKS

OVERALL CHALLENGE
| LOW | MID | HIGH | SUPER HIGH |

The implementation obstacles seem high, because the product has to be adapted to the specific needs and language of this market, and accessing it will require special efforts

We estimated that investors will adopt our product only after it was proven to be successful in start-ups, and hence the time to revenue is relatively long

The risks are relatively high due to competitive threat and barriers of adoption

The overall rating of each market opportunity could now be depicted on the Attractiveness Map, to help us characterise and compare our options:

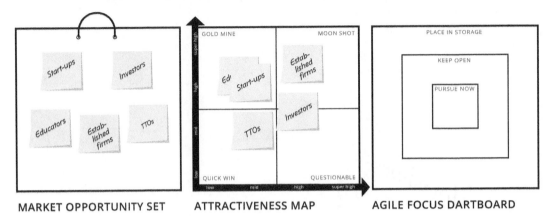

MARKET OPPORTUNITY SET　　**ATTRACTIVENESS MAP**　　**AGILE FOCUS DARTBOARD**

According to the map, start-ups and educators are both Gold Mine opportunities. Established firms are a Moon Shot opportunity and TTOs are Quick Wins. Investors are somewhat in the middle.

We decided that start-ups would thus be our Primary Market Opportunity.
It was now time to understand how other market opportunities are connected to our primary one, so that we can build a smart portfolio around it.

Next, we used Worksheet 3 to design our Agile Focus Strategy.

Educators are the most attractive opportunity next to start-ups. This opportunity is highly related to start-ups – both in terms of the product and the market, so that we can increase our value with relatively low efforts. We decided to pursue this Growth Option in parallel to our primary market.

Technology Transfer Offices were analysed next. Our product would need to be somewhat adapted to turn into a screening tool, and hence the product relatedness is at a medium level, and so is the market relatedness, as start-ups and TTOs require different channels and not necessarily reference each other. Still, TTOs can serve as a Growth Option, and we decided to keep it open for later.

Established firms seem to bear high potential for our tool. The product they require is somewhat related to the product for start-ups, but the markets have low relatedness. While this opportunity can become a promising Growth Option in the future, it can also serve as our Backup Option – if we fail to succeed with entrepreneurs. We decided to keep it open.

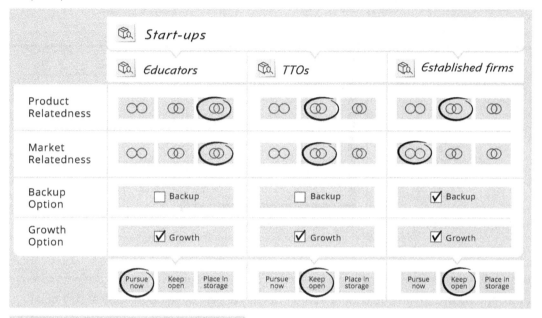

Lastly, we looked at **investors**. While the product needed to be adapted and thus is only somewhat related, the market relatedness to start-ups was tight, as they both share extensive word-of-mouth.

This opportunity could help us grow in the future, so we decided to keep it open as well.

Finally, it was time to gather all these decisions and depict our strategy on the Dartboard: we would focus on pursuing start-ups and educators, keep TTOs and investors open for future growth, and keep established firms open as a Backup Option.

Here is how the Navigator's Navigator looks like:

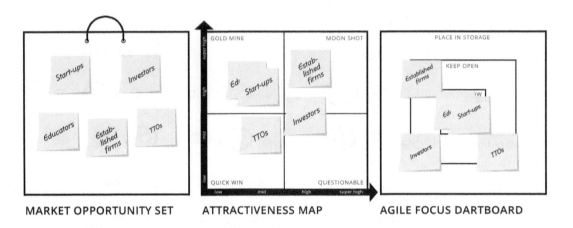

MARKET OPPORTUNITY SET   **ATTRACTIVENESS MAP**   **AGILE FOCUS DARTBOARD**

Based on this decision, we tailored the tool to entrepreneurs and decided to write this book and record an on-line course at the outset. We also developed several curricula programmes to address educators in parallel.

Overall, our own Agile Focus Strategy helped us not only in building our roadmap, but also in shaping our marketing materials and key messages.

Now it's YOUR turn to find out where to play. Apply the Navigator to make sure that you are running in the right direction and remain agile without losing your focus!

These worksheets are for you . . .

THE MARKET OPPORTUNITY NAVIGATOR

NAME

DATE

MARKET OPPORTUNITY SET

1 Use Worksheet 1 to identify potential market opportunities, and place them in the set

ATTRACTIVENESS MAP

2 Use Worksheet 2 to evaluate the attractiveness of each market opportunity, and place each one on the map

GOLD MINE

MOON SHOT

QUICK WIN

QUESTIONABLE

POTENTIAL

Low Mid High Super High

CHALLENGE

Low Mid High Super High

AGILE FOCUS DARTBOARD

3 Use Worksheet 3 to design your Agile Focus Strategy, and mark it on the Dartboard

PLACE IN STORAGE

KEEP OPEN

PURSUE NOW

market opportunity = any combination of application + customer

Use sticky notes to represent each market opportunity

WORKSHEET 1
GENERATE YOUR MARKET OPPORTUNITY SET

List the venture's core abilities or technological elements

Characterise them based on their functions and properties. Describe them in a general manner, independent from your (envisioned) product.

ABILITIES

Identify your market opportunities

Which applications can you offer with your core abilities? Which customers may need them? Zoom in to further segment each customer group.

APPLICATIONS

CUSTOMERS

application **+** customer **=** market opportunity

Place the market opportunities that you would like to evaluate in the Market Opportunity Set.

2 □ WORKSHEET 2

EVALUATE MARKET OPPORTUNITY ATTRACTIVENESS

Use this worksheet for every market opportunity you would like to evaluate.

 Market Opportunity:

POTENTIAL

| LOW | MID | HIGH | SUPER HIGH |

COMPELLING REASON TO BUY
Unmet need
Effective solution
Better than current solutions

| LOW | MID | HIGH | SUPER HIGH |

MARKET VOLUME
Current market size
Expected growth

| LOW | MID | HIGH | SUPER HIGH |

ECONOMIC VIABILITY
Margins (value vs. cost)
Customers' ability to pay
Customer stickiness

OVERALL POTENTIAL

| LOW | MID | HIGH | SUPER HIGH |

CHALLENGE

| LOW | MID | HIGH | SUPER HIGH |

IMPLEMENTATION OBSTACLES
Product development difficulties
Sales and distribution difficulties
Funding challenges

| LOW | MID | HIGH | SUPER HIGH |

TIME TO REVENUE
Development time
Time between product and market readiness
Length of sale cycle

| LOW | MID | HIGH | SUPER HIGH |

EXTERNAL RISKS
Competitive threat
Third party dependencies
Barriers to adoption

OVERALL CHALLENGE

| LOW | MID | HIGH | SUPER HIGH |

 Use the overall ratings to situate each market opportunity on the Attractiveness Map.

WORKSHEET 3

3 DESIGN YOUR AGILE FOCUS STRATEGY

Build a smart portfolio around your Primary Market Opportunity to mitigate your risk and increase your value.

I. Choose a Primary Market Opportunity to focus on (based on the Attractiveness Map).

II. Pick other attractive market opportunities from your set to examine possible Backup and Growth Options.

Relatedness to your Primary Market Opportunity:

PRODUCT RELATEDNESS
To what extent do the products share: technological competences, required resources, necessary networks

MARKET RELATEDNESS
To what extent do the customers share: values and benefits, sales channels, word-of-mouth

Suitable as:

BACKUP OPTION
Attractive market opportunities that do not share major risks with your Primary Market Opportunity to allow for a change in direction

☐ Backup

☐ Backup

☐ Backup

GROWTH OPTION
Attractive market opportunities that allow your business to create additional value

☐ Growth

☐ Growth

☐ Growth

III. Design your Agile Focus Strategy:

- Keep at least one Backup and one Growth Option open
- Decide if any option is worth pursuing now
- Place the rest in storage

Pursue now	Keep open	Place in storage

Pursue now	Keep open	Place in storage

Pursue now	Keep open	Place in storage

Mark your strategy on the Agile Focus Dartboard.

Thank you note

Writing this book involved a great amount of feedback, iterations and testing. In particular, we wish to thank the following persons for their invaluable feedback and inspiring discussions over the years: Ayala Berenson, Tali Hadasa Blank, Bart Clarysse, Erwin Danneels, Shirah Foy, Marc Gandillon, Uzi de Haan, Yonathan Lerner, Ian MacMillan, John Mullins, Argyro Nikiforou, Alex Osterwalder, Nettra Pan, Yves Pigneur, Keren Rubin, Galia Schwartz, Gal Shaul, Jana Thiel, James Thompson and Saar Yoskovitz. You helped us shape the ideas presented in this book and for that we are more than grateful!

We also owe our gratitude to those who have helped make this book a reality. Specifically, we are grateful for the support of our publisher and, in particular, of Eloise Cook and her professional team. We also owe a huge thank you to our designer, Dana Shimoni, who accompanied us from the very first outline to the very last detail of this book. Dana – you are the best!

Last, but of course not least, we wish to thank our families for their never-ending support throughout the years. Writing a book is a long journey and you walked it with us, providing a tremendous amount of encouragement and inspiration. This book would not have happened without you!

Index